STUDY & ANSWER GUIDE
by W. O. Loescher for the Book
DR. MARTIN LUTHER (1483 – 1546)

The original biography was issued in 1883 by the late Professor August L. Graebner in German, under the title: **Dr. Martin Luther** (At that time Prof. Graebner was serving as seminary professor of the Synod of Wisconsin. The German version of the book is now in Public Domain). This **Study Guide** is in reference to the translatoin of this book.

© 2015 Quotations for reviews or even for teaching situations are allowed. Otherwise, all publication rights are reserved without prior permission from the publisher, currently W.O. Loescher.

ISBN 978-0-359-08012-0

This STUDY GUIDE, for 48 Chapters of the book, Dr. Martin Luther 1483-1546, offers:

Part 1: Summary for each of the 48 Chapters with:
    a. Some Names of Persons and Places in each Chapter
    b. Followed by Chapter Summary, and
    c. Followed by Questions about Contents of the Chapter

Part 2: Four Approximation Maps
Part 3: Suggested Answers for questions in the chapters

The Roman numerals at the beginning of each chapter indicate how the teaching material in this Study Guide may be condensed into 24 sections. Optional: Any limited number of chapters may be selected for shorter group studies.

Wholesome Use of the "Answer Guide" Section

1. Begin each chapter study with appropriate prayer.
2. Attentively read the given Chapter(s) with grateful heart and open mind.
3. Write your own answer into the "Study Guide - Questions" blank lines (pp. 1-89) before you look up the answer in the "Answer Section") (pp. 95-131).
4. Compare your answer with the suggested answer in the "Answer Guide" to find out:
    a. whether you have missed something
    b. or you are able to supply something that had been missed in the "Answer Section"
5. Compare your final answer with someone else's answer with whom you have partnered for this venture: a friend, or a larger study group.
6. Add fitting question(s) in addition to the one's supplied in the "Study Guide" section.
7. Thank our Triune God for the blessing of Christian fellowship in context with joint discussion sessions about our Lutheran heritage.

I General Introduction for the Dr. Martin Luther Biography

A. About the author of the book only (not the Study Guide): See the pages in the introductory section of the book under the headings, "FOREWORD", followed by, "ABOUT THE ORIGINAL AUTHOR".

B. The original title of the book was <u>Dr. Martin Luther</u>. The new title is as it is shown on the title page of this Study Guide.

C. About the approximate first half of the life of Dr. Martin Luther:
   1. Luther's school training: to the age of 13 at Mansfeld; to the age of 14 at Magdeburg; to the age of 17 at Eisenach; to the age of 21 at the U of Erfurt; to the age of 24 in the monastery at Erfurt; at the age of 23 Luther was ordained as priest; at the age of 29 he received the Dr. of Theology title; at the age of 34 he wrote the first draft of the 95 Theses; at the age of 49 the publication of the Luther Bible.
   2. From about the age of 27 Luther was led to rely more and more on Holy Scripture as the absolute truth for theology and the Christian faith. He kept learning ever more about Jesus as his Savior from **all** his sins. The book tells how Luther kept sharing the treasures of God's Word.

D. In regard to the 500th anniversary of the Lutheran reformation.
   1. October 31, 1517, is usually recognized as the spark with which the Almighty God ignited the reformation movement.
   2. However, the overall purpose of the Reformation was really nothing less than our God's providing the translation of the Bible, God's infallible Word, into common language in Germany at that time, which was being accomplished during the years 1512-1534. Revisions of the same translation also kept being made in the editions of 1541, 1543, and 1545. Translations into other languages kept increasing in following years and centuries. God keeps providing opportunity to his people of all cultures to benefit from better understanding of His Law, and His precious gift of His Gospel.

I **Questions** for further discussion in regard to "The General Introduction"

1. (A) What is the "Public Domain"?

2. Find out how the concept of registering copyright applies to books in the Public Domain.

3. React to the last five lines of the first paragraph under FOREWORD on p. I in the first section of the book:

4. What is "**L**uther's **V**olksbibliothek", or, "People's Luther Library", abbreviated as "L.V."
   See the last paragraph of p. II, for an answer

5. What might you say is a major difference between Dr. Martin Luther and Dr. Martin Luther King?

6. How might Luther's education years compare with basic education years in our current pastor track education

systems?

7. Was there another draft of the 95 Theses? Yes! Do you know what it was called?

8. What is a sad reality about the first half of Martin Luther's life?

9. What is a usual secular assessment of Luther's place in N.T. history?

10. What is of first importance of Luther's role in all of N.T. history?

11. What may we regard was the main need for the 16th century Reformation?

II Chapters 1-3 - Luther's Early Upbringing,
II Chapter 1 - Luther's Ancestors and Parents

Names and Places in Chapter 1

Hans and Margaret Luther	- Martin Luther's parents
Henry Luther	- Hans Luther's father, Paternal Grandfather of Martin Luther
Margaret Luther, nee Zigurin	- Hans Luther's mother, Paternal Grandmother of Martin Luther (or Ziegler)
Jacob Luther	- Close brother of Martin Luther, (one of 6 siblings)
Moehra, several km. southwest of Eisenach, in the region of Thueringia	- First home of Hans and Margaret Luther, where Martin was born

Summary of Chapter 1

A. His father and grandfather, Hans and Heinz (or Henry), poor farmers in the area of Moehra, Thuringia, could at times also be called ruffians.

B. Variations of the name "Luther"; Hans Luther and his wife moved to Eisleben which was located in the County of Mansfeld.

C. Ancestry is provided of Martin Luther's mother, Margaret ("Greta or Maggie").
  (See p. 2 in the book – the last paragraph)

D. Eisleben was the place where Martin was born and baptized.

E. The family moved to Mansfeld in 1484. He would be one of 7 children in due time.

F. Discipline was applied in their home. Read about the incident of having taken a nut.

G. It was evident that spiritual darkness was prevailing under papal religion.

H. Martin did not learn about Jesus as his Savior from all his sins during his childhood years.

Questions for Chapter 1

1. (# C) Graebner points out that Martin's grandmother was a Lindemann; his mother was a "Zigur", or as the name is also found, "Ziegler".

2. How old was Martin Luther, when he was baptized?

3. What does this tell us about Martin's parents?

4. (#F) For what was Martin once punished severely as a child?

5. During later years what was Luther's "familiar advice" for disciplining children?

6. (# G) What evidence did Prof. Graebner supply about the then-existing spiritual darkness?

II Chapter 2 - Martin's Youth Years at Mansfeld, Magdeburg, and Eisenach.

Names and Places in Chapter 2

Nicolaus Oemler	- Friend of Luther, a little older than Martin, who would sometimes carry Martin to their elementary school in Mansfeld
Hans Reinicke	- Childhood school friend of Martin in Mansfeld
Mansfeld	- Childhood home town of Martin where he received his elementary education
Magdeburg	- The town where Martin continued going to school for one year at the age of 13-14. The school was run by the Nollbrueder semi-monastic fellowship, also known as Brothers of the Common Life.
Wenzeslaus Link	- Became a closer school friend of Martin during schooling at Magdeburg. This friendship continued into the reformation years.
Eisenach	- about 45-50 miles southwest of Eisleben, where Martin attended school at the age of 14-17.
Johannes Trebonius	- Dedicated principal of the school at Eisenach
Konrad (or Kunz) and Ursula Cotta	- A nobility family in Eisenach, who welcomed Martin in their home

Summary of Chapter 2

A. Martin's elementary schooling was very harsh. Martin knew Christ only as his strict and angry judge. Yet, he also did learn some good things.

B. In 1497 Martin was sent to a much better school at Magdeburg. Note the example of the self-righteous holiness of Count Anhalt..

C. Note Martin's experiences as beggar for bread, and also his having a high fever.

D. The gospel of Christ could be known by some, as Count Guenther indicated when dying. (See Romans 10:18, 20)

E. After one year at Magdeburg Martin was sent to an even better school at Eisenach. There he attended school for three years. Note his good experience of being befriended by the Kunz Cotta family.

F. Note the noble character of teacher Trebonius.

G. Luther learned Latin in that school, but he did not hear the gospel.

Questions for Chapter 2

1. (# A) How did Martin Luther later in life describe his teacher and elementary school at Mansfeld?

2. (# B) Describe the example of "grizzled holiness" as Count Anhalt showed with his life style?

3. (# D) Why would we thank God for closure of physical life like that of Count Guenther?

4. (# F) Note the noble character of teacher Trebonius. How did his high respect for his students become fulfilled in regard to Martin Luther later in life?

II Chapter 3 - Luther at the University of Erfurt

Names and Places in Chapter 3

Erfurt — The city in which Luther attended the university for four years
Jodocus Trutvetter — A more famous scholastic star on the faculty at the university
Musicus — Luther's nickname as lute playing fellowship leader

Summary of Chapter 3

A. The father wanted his son to become a lawyer. Therefore he now sent him to the well reputed University of Erfurt. The education procedure was: 1st year, general philosophy, after that, study in one or more "majors", - Law for Martin.
B. Valid scholarship required becoming efficient in scholasticism. Martin became a model student. The ancient Greek and Roman philosophy masters had also become regarded highly and were recently imported for study at the University of Erfurt. Luther could not yet learn Greek.
C. By the age of 19 Martin had earned the Baccalaureus of Philosophy degree.
D. Martin discovered a Bible – What a surprise! Martin's accident of cutting through one of his arteries shows the immense fear he carried. He had been a diligent and reputable student. He also picked up lute playing while he was laid up.
E. His father always continued to support him. But now, what happened?

Questions for Chapter 3

1. (# A) Why did educators divide the subjects taught in grade levels in universities as they did?

2. (# B) Why was the need of learning Greek so important for the work Luther would do in his life?

3. (# D) What was the big surprise for Martin?

4. (# D) How did the ability of playing the lute enhance Martin's life?

5. (# E) Why did Martin's becoming a monk affect Martin's father so negatively?

III Chapter 4 - Martin Luther at the Augustinian Monastery

Names and Places in Chapter 4

Augustinian Monastery of Erfurt	- Where Martin lived as a monk for three years
Johannes von Lasphe	- The bishop who ordained Luther as priest in 1507
John Hus (1369-1415)	- Bohemian Reformer in Prague (See chapter 17 in the Study Guide)

Summary of Chapter 4

A. What people were thinking about monasteries:

B. As a lightning bolt struck next to Martin, he was greatly frightened and made a vow. Martin became a monk.

C. A monk's set of clothing; Martin's first six months; His own first Bible; his threefold vow; his many holy works: castigation of body, night vigils, fasting, readings, confessions. Not any of these could bring him comfort.

D. False grace of God and deceptive righteousness that were being taught did not help him.

E. The actual words as they, as monks, would sell their good works to other people:

F. Staupitz, the prior of the monastery, did at times offer him some good counsel, pointing to the central message of Scripture about the true meaning of repentance, also about his eternal election, about hope for a Christian, and about forgiveness of sins.

G. Note Luther's confusion, when he read from a book by John Hus:

H. Martin had become well versed in regard to writings by scholastic authors, but also in regard to the writings of other philosophers.

I. Luther remained a staunch defender of the papacy and its religious system.

Question about Chapter 4

1. (# A) What were the people thinking about monasteries?

2. Why would such thoughts seem so natural that monastic life provides a higher degree of holiness?

3. (# C) Why couldn't the monastery requirements bring any comfort to Martin Luther? (Re. C above)

4. (# D) Lets do a little in-class reading from pp. 17-18

5. Note the father–son conversation after Luther's consecration as priest?

6. (# E) Find the words with which the monks would sell their good works to others.?

7. (# F) Let's do some more reading about Staupitz counseling Luther with true gospel gems about:

    repentance;

    election;

    hope;

    forgiveness of sins;

8. (#G) Why did the book which John Hus had written confuse Luther?

IV Chapters 5-8 - Luther's First Years from His Wittenberg Base
IV Chapter 5 - Beginnings at Wittenberg as Professor and Preacher

Names and Places in Chapter 5

Frederick the Wise — Head of government in Saxony, and one of seven electors. It was the responsibility of only 6 selected counts to elect the new empire Caesar in 1519. The standing rule had been that 7 electors would do this,

Wittenberg — A city on the Elbe River, northwest of Dresden, where the elector decided to begin a university in 1502.

Dr. Staupitz — Deacon of the University of Wittenberg. He drafted Luther from the Erfurt Augustinian Monastery to the University of Wittenberg in 1508 to teach religion in line with scholastic procedure.

Summary of Chapter 5

A. The University of Wittenberg began in 1502 with Dr. Pollich and Dr. Staupitz put in charge for putting together the first faculty. The latter could also draft gifted monks. This university was to be financed as a foundation (a kind of a federation made up of area congregations).

B. Three more served on the faculty: Trutvetter, Carlstadt, and Amsdorf. By 1515 several more had been added. Martin Luther was one of these who had been added in 1508. Martin had wanted to teach Holy Scripture but had to start as teacher of scholastics.

C. Luther became baccalaureate for teaching Holy Scripture in March, 1509, then sententiarist. His next step was becoming licentiate, and then doctor, to qualify for full professorship.

Questions about Chapter 5

1. (# A) Why did enrollment at the U of Wittenberg drop so drastically the first 4 years?

2. (# A) How did Elector Frederick succeed in boosting financial support for his University?

3. (# B) What was the starting salary for Martin as a member of the faculty of the University?

4. (#C) Can you name the four steps that had to be taken to attain the Doctor title? (# C above)

IV Chapter 6 - Luthers Trip to Rome

Names and Places in Chapter 6

Bavaria — A government territory in South Germany

Pope Julius II — Head of Roman Catholicism, when Luther made his trip to Rome.

Summary of Chapter 6

A. Staupitz selected Martin to obtain counsel from the pope for settling a dispute among the Augustinian monks. Martin and another monk started out in 1511.

B. In Italy they lodged at various libertine monasteries. At one of these the attempt by other monks to kill them was thwarted by the gatekeeper.

C. Martin was deeply dismayed as he witnessed all kinds of debauchery, corruption, and blasphemy in Rome. Pope Julius II seemed interested mainly in wars and hunts rather than in church business. Luther valued this insight highly during later years of his life.

D. Martin wanted to gain special credit in respect to so called purgatory on Pilate's Staircase.

E. Martin derived no comfort from any of these doings. One special Bible passage accompanied Luther to and from Rome, namely, "The righteous will live by faith."

Questions about Chapter 6

1. (# A) By what means did the two monks travel to Rome?

2. (# A) About what had the Augustinian monks been arguing?

3. (# B) What got the two travelling monks into serious trouble at one of the Italian monasteries?

4. (# C) What is "debauchery" in Galatians 5:19 (NIV), and how does this word apply to Question 3?

5. (# D) What was "Pilate's Staircase" claimed to be? What good was it supposed to provide?

6. (# E) What Bible passage had the Holy Spirit implanted into Martin's heart and mind as travelling companion to and from Rome? For an expanded study of this travelling companion you may look up Romans 1:17; Habakkuk 2:3-4; Galatians 3:11; Hebrews 10:37-39; et. al. (et. al. = and others)

IV Chapter 7 - Luther Being Awarded the Doctor Title

A. After returning from Rome, Martin kept preaching in the dilapidated chapel of the monastery. Running out of space soon, he had to be moved into the pulpit of the parish church. Staupitz wanted Martin to go after the doctor title. However, he had to first convince him in the under-the-pear-tree event with a special command!"

B. Martin received licentiate degree October 4, 1512. The doctor title came shortly after that on October 19, 1512. The candidate had to write and submit a number of theses for debate. Also, note Luther's impressive list for qualifying for a doctorate..

Questions about Chapter 7

1. (# A) Why did Staupitz's command to "obey" have such powerful influence on Martin so that he proceeded to study for his doctor title?

2. (# A) Why had Martin tried to decline the directive to study for doctor title?

3. (# B) Of what did the examination consist to attain a doctor title? Again, note the progression up to that stage: (baccalaureate, sententiarist, licentiate, doctor)

4. (# B) Let's read a list of Martin Luther's qualifications for receiving the doctor title:

IV Chapter 8 - Luther's Increasing Activity as Professor, Preacher and Supervisor (1512 – 1517)

Names and Places in Chapter 8

Wenzeslaus Link	- Luther's old acquaintance and brother monk
Trutvetter	- Professor who was moved from the U of Erfurt to the U of Wittenberg.
Carlstadt, Andreas von Bodenstein	- Replacement for Trutvetter on the Wittenberg faculty
Georg Burkhard	- Student with Luther at Erfurt; studied law and served as magistrate.
Spalatin, the same as Georg Burkhard	- He later became court chaplain at the castle and served as mediator between Elector Frederick the Wise and Luther
John Lange	- Fellow professor at Wittenberg and closer friend of Luther
John Tetzel	- Dominican monk who started selling indulgences in neighboring towns of Wittenberg in boastful manner in 1516.

Summary of Chapter 8

A. Note Dr. Pollich's prediction about Martin Luther.

B. From the year 1515 on, co-workers of Luther at the University included Pollich, Staupitz, Carlstadt, Link, Burkhard, and Lange.

C. Samples from Luther's lectures on the Psalms:

   1. He connected Psalm 32:1 with Holy Scripture's own interpretation of Romans 4:6-8. (Ps. 32:1 in the NIV translation, "Blessed is he whose transgressions are forgiven, whose sins are covered.")

   2. Psalm 61:8 is Psalm 61:7 in the NIV translation and states, "May he (*namely, the king*) be enthroned in God's presence forever; appoint your love and faithfulness to him to protect him."

   3. Psalm 51:11, which is Ps. 51:9 in the NIV translation, states, "Hide your face from my sins and blot out all my iniquity."

D. In 1515 Luther began to lecture on Paul's Epistle to the Romans, in 1516 on Paul's Epistle to Galatians.

E. Luther began to understand Scripture's meaning of righteousness ever better, as can be realized from his excellent letter in 1516 to his former school friend, Spenlein. (May be read in class.)

F. Luther became quite excited when he found the book which was written by Johannes Tauler in regard to gospel preaching. Tauler had lived a couple centuries before Luther.

G. Luther began to distinguish between law and gospel ever more clearly. He issued the booklet, "The Seven Penitential Psalms with German Commentary" (6, 32, 38, 51, 102, 130, 143.)

H. The late Professor A. Graebner, author of this biography of Luther, gives us an example of Luther's earlier more stilted translation of Psalm 130 (translated into English by the translator of these words in approximate terminology).

I. Luther was then also given the added duty of serving as district vicar in the 12 monasteries of Meissen and Thueringia. Notice his overloaded work schedule at that time.

J. Carlstadt, being required to return from Rome to Wittenberg, found Luther's teaching considerably changed from what was common Roman teaching procedure.

K. What are disputations? They are actually debates set up with previously published statements, or theses. Learn from an example of 7 theses as they had been set up by Franz Guenther, one of Dr. Martin Luther's students.

Questions about Chapter 8

1. (# A) What were Dr. Pollich's two predictions about Luther?

2. (# C & D) Which were the first 3 books of the Bible on which Luther based his lectures?

3. (# E) Let's read Luther's letter to his friend Spenlein in 1516. What begins to become more clear in regard to Martin's understanding about righteousness from this letter?

4. (# I) What were some of the duties of Luther as District Vicar?

5. (# J) How did Carlstadt, returning from Rome, find Luther's lecturing differ from former status quo?

6. (# K) Read the example of the seven theses from Franz Guenther's disputation for Baccalaureus to get an idea of how the sentences in a disputation (debate) were set up:

V Chapters 9 - 10 - Having Revealed His Gospel to Luther, God Led Him into Action

Consider previous attempts at Reformation in France, Italy, Bohemia, and in England.

V Chapter 9 - The 95 Theses

Names and Places in Chapter 9

Nicea — The city where the Nicene Creed had been adopted in 325 a.D. There the system of imposing penances, in its earlier stages, had also kept being regulated. This system later led to the deeply corrupted system of selling indulgences.

Leo X (1513-1522 a.D.) — Pope on the Roman Catholic throne, who sponsored the selling of indulgences to raise money for the church system.

Archbishop Albrecht of Mainz — Luther informed him and Scultetus, his bishop in the Brandenburg area, before he posted the 95 Theses.

Summary of Chapter 9

A. A historic summary is given of how purgatory gradually became coupled with indulgences.

B. Archbishop Albrecht of Mainz & Magdeburg, under direction of Pope Leo X, commissioned John Tetzel as one of the agents to sell indulgences in Germany, as forgiveness of sins.

C. Luther aired out his dismay as he kept hearing about Tetzel's destructive spiritual propaganda not far from Wittenberg.

D. Luther informed Hieronymus Scultetus of Brandenburg, his overseer, and scolded Archbishop Albrecht with copies of some of his theses and a special letter.

E. Some of the 95 Theses:

1. The 1st and the last 2 theses set the stage with the topic of true repentance.
2. Thesis 5: Luther defends the pope.
3. Theses 8-11: Punishment should be applied only to the living.
4. Thesis 21: Luther attacks boastful indulgence peddlers.
5. Thesis 27: Luther defines indulgences as teachings of man.
6. Thesis 35: Luther calls the area indulgence peddler a false teacher.
7. Thesis 39: Such selling forgiveness undermined the work of sincere preachers.
8. Theses 41-46: Luther distinguished between indulgences and works of compassion.
9. Thesis 47: Christians are not commanded to buy indulgences.
10. Theses 53-55: Against the pomp and ceremonies in the selling of indulgences, and the silencing God's Word in the process.
11. Theses 62-64: Luther exposes the so-called treasure of good works from the saints of the past in light of the true treasure, the gospel.
12. Theses 71-74: Luther was still defending indulgences, the pope, and purgatory. (Luther later corrected himself.

F. The dream of Elector Frederick the Wise.

Questions about Chapter 9

1. (# A) If a person should want to divide the development of the teaching of purgatory into five segments, which would these be?

2. (# B) How and why did Archbishop Albrecht, in charge of the R.C. expanded district of Mainz, seek to promote the indulgence sales in his district?

3. (# B & C) How was John Tetzel proceeding with his assignment?

4. (# C) Why did Martin Luther become so upset about the selling of indulgences?

5. (# C) What was the treasure of relics in the castle church of Wittenberg?

6. (# D) Who was bishop Scultetus?

7. (# D) About what did Dr. Luther rebuke Archbishop Albrecht?

8. (# E.) With what main Bible doctrine did Dr. M. Luther begin the 95 Theses?

9. (# E. 12) What false teachings was Dr. Luther still defending in the 95 Theses? Note how Martin Luther explained this himself later, when he burned a copy of the papal bull.

10. (# E) Name at least 5 issues from this list of highlights with which Dr. Luther properly defended Bible teachings as you know them.

11. (# E) Besides the exposure of false repentance, what was a main evil exposed with the 95 Theses according to your opinion?

12. (# F) Why is the legendary dream of Elector Frederick so fitting for this whole event?

V Chapter 10 - Early Consequences of the Publication of the 95 Theses

Names and Places in Chapter 10

Silvester Mazolini — Roman Catholic censor of books at the time of the posting of the 95 Theses

Summary of Chapter 10

 A. Copies were circulating throughout Germany in about two weeks.
 B. Excitement was seen in monasteries and everywhere.
 C. Some critics thought it would lead to a repeat of Kostnitz. (About Kostnitz see the "Point of Information" under the outline for chapter 17, of this compendium.)
 D. Luther was perplexed, - no debaters - He stood alone.
 E. Tetzel turned to Archbishop Albrecht for help but to no avail.
 F. Tetzel got some help from the Dominican, Wimpina.
 G. A document by a top theologian of Rome against Luther puzzled him.
 H. Luther just kept on writing explanations of the Theses with a writing: "A Sermon about Indulgences and Grace."
 I. Luther kept depending on Scripture ever more.
 J. Luther provided a comforting interpretation of Psalm 110 for a friend.

Questions about Chapter 10

1. (# C) What was the Kostnitz affair? (See a description of it on p. 30 of this "Study & Answer Guide" under "Some Background Information".)

2. (# E & F) From what 2 men did John Tetzel seek to get help for answering Luther's charges?

3. (# G) Why was Martin Luther startled when he received the document from Sylvester Mazolini of Prierio?

4. (# H) How did Martin Luther follow through during the following months with promoting the central issues of the 95 Theses?

5. (# J) Why did Dr. Martin Luther's interpretation of Psalm 110 fit so well into this time period?

6. (# I) From what source did Luther derive ever more increasing support for telling the whole truth to the world?

VI Chapters 11 - 13 - Controversy Picks up for the Cause of the Reformation
VI Chapter 11 - Luther at Heidelberg

Names and Places in Chapter 11

Heidelberg — The city where an Augustinian Convention was held in 1518. Luther was also asked to present a set of theses for debate.

Bucer, Martin — A Dominican monk, who attended the Heidelberg Convention and was very impressed with Luther's exceptional theses presentation.

Summary of Chapter 11

This convention might be regarded as a preparatory forerun for the later key debate at Leipzig.

    A. Luther was welcomed at this convention of Augustinians in a spirit of excitement.
    B. Two of Luther's theses provide a clear picture about his theology.
    C. Dominican Martin Bucer gave a glowing testimonial about Luther.
    D. Luther traveled back to Wittenberg to continue his work, arriving May 15, 1518.

Questions about Chapter 11

1. (# A) What was the general agenda for the Augustinian Convention at Heidelberg?

2. (# B) What item did they add to their agenda, since M. Luther would be attending?

3. (# B) What became clear to all attendees about Dr. Luther's theology from the 2 theses of his disputation as they are quoted?

4. (# C) In what way was the Dominican monk, Martin Bucer, impressed about Luther?

5. (# D) Why did Elector Frederick want Luther back in Wittenberg as soon as possible?

VI Chapter 12 - Luther Begins Striking back Verbally against Attackers

Names and Places in Chapter 12

Wimpina — A Dominican monk in the Frankfurt, Germany area, whom Tetzel used to back his convoluted theses against Luther

Jacob von Hoogstraten — Another Dominican, who jumped into the fray with shoddy writing, condemning Luther as a heretic. Luther set him straight thoroughly.

Summary of Chapter 12

A. Dr. Eck's "Obilisks" against the 95 Theses: Carlstadt answered Eck with a challenge to debate, while Luther was still at Heidelberg.
B. Luther kept working on his "Resolutions" and sent copies to the Bishop of Brandenburg and to the pope together with a remarkable Letter to the pope.
C. Luther really tore into Tetzel for his flimsy Scripture-distorting response to Luther's "Sermon about Indulgence and Grace."
D. Luther's scathing rebuke of the Dominican Jacob von Hoogstraten.

Questions about Chapter 12

1. (# A) What was Dr. Carlstadt's objective in challenging Dr. Eck to a debate?

2. (# B) Why did Dr. Luther send a copy of his Resolutions to the Bishop of Brandenburg?

3. (# B) Let's read Dr. Luther's remarkable letter to the pope which he sent along with a copy of his Resolutions:

4. (# B) Though Martin Luther would submit to the pope in almost everything, what was he not willing to take back?

5. (# C) What was it that upset Martin Luther so much about John Tetzel's criticism?

6. (# D) How did Luther completely destroy the criticism of Jacob von Hoogstraten?

VI Chapter 13 - Summons to Rome
Names and Places in Chapter 13

Silvester Prierias — Silvester Prierias, first challenger in the Curia Romana to assess the then so called Luther heresy. He was one of the appointed judges for this case.

Philip Melanchthon — At the age of 21 he was called to serve as the new Greek Professor at the U. of Wittenberg.

Summary of Chapter 13

A. Pope Leo X expressed his disapproval of Luther's action beyond mere controversy with his actions at Rome and with a message to Elector Frederick. Martin Luther received the summons on August 7, 1518 to come to Rome within 60 days.

B. Dr. Luther showed disappointment as he realized the pope's real intentions. He then answered Dr. Eck's Obelisks with his "Asterisks" writing.

C. In anticipation of a ban from Rome Dr. Luther preached a "Sermon in regard to the Ban" to prepare and calm the congregation, including the Elector, for what may happen. When he received the summons, he recalled that sermon from memory and put it into writing for wider circulation.

D. Martin wrote to Staupitz, expressing his fear in regard to his former teacher and friend. Staupitz responded with a comforting letter.

E. The Wittenberg faculty and student body stood in support of Luther.

F. Philip Melanchthon was added to the Wittenberg faculty. Note his exceptional skills, which had been developed from his childhood.

Questions about Chapter 13

1. (# A) How did Pope Leo X show his real intentions with his action at Rome?

2. (# B) Note why Luther had not given an answer to Eck's Obelisks right away.

3. (# B) With what document did Luther later answer Eck's Obelisks?

4. (# B) Cite at least two points which Luther scored in his answer:

5. (# C) Cite a couple points Luther scored in his "Sermon regarding the Ban":

6. (# E) How many of the Wittenberg faculty and student body did not stand with Luther?

7. (# E) For what action did Luther seriously punish the Wittenberg students from the pulpit?

8. (# F) How might Melanchthon's joining the Wittenberg faculty be viewed in comparison with Aaron's and Hur's actions as recorded in Exodus 17:10?

VII Chapter 14 - Cajetan - Rome Becoming Aggressive

Names and Places in Chapter 14

Cardinal Gaeta	- He served as papal legate (ambassador) in Augsburg for a so called hearing of Martin Luther. He was also known as Cardinal Cajetan.
Carmelite Monastery at Augsburg	- Luther transferred there for lodging some time after his arrival in Augsburg.
Link	- Friend, co-traveler, and message conveyer for Luther at Augsburg
Spalatin	- The mediator between Frederick the Wise and Luther Staupitz
	- Luther's former prior at Erfurt. He had moved from Wittenberg to Salzburg, when the reformation proceedings were getting hotter. Luther still regarded him as an old friend who had helped him in critical situations at the Augustinian monastery at Erfurt.
Pirkheimer, Bilibald	- An educated and quite well-versed knight, who offered shelter for Luther after Luther left Augsburg in that forced night journey.

Summary of Chapter 14

A. Eector Frederick was of central importance to Rome, but also to Luther. The Elector wanted Luther to be allowed to debate on German soil. The pope granted this request to take place in Augsburg under the legate Cajetan's jurisdiction.

B. Note that Luther's God-given determination to travel to Augsburg was very high, even though previous reformers had provided a bad track record for survival.

C. About the end of September, 1518, once in Augsburg, Luther held off accepting the invitation to see Cardinal Cajetan right away, but under good advice waited for an official document from Caesar for this purpose. In the meantime Luther had transferred to a Carmelite monastery on October 7th. Caesar document arrived Oct. 11th.

D. Oct. 12th: The meeting with the cardinal began.
  1. The bone of contention: Two statements, one from the 95 Theses, the other from Luther's Resolutions.
  2. TheCardinal continued to request: "Recant!" When they had reached an impasse, the cardinal declared a recess for one day to think things over.

E. Oct. 13th: Luther returned accompanied by five counselors and a notary. It was his proposal to:
  1. Either the cardinal allow debate of his questioned statements then and there, or
  2. That this debate be allowed to take place somewhere else, or
  3. Submit his statements to one of four named universities for a verdict, or
  4. Submit his position in writing to be submitted to the pope.

F. The Cardinal stubbornly kept insisting, "Recant!" Due to Staupitz's appeal, the Cardinal finally agreed to receive Luther's statements in writing.

G. Oct. 14th: Luther presented his position "with crystal clarity". After heated controversial discussion the cardinal just kept repeating his command, "Recant!

H. Oct. 15th: Luther reported the proceedings of the last meeting to Spalatin by way of a letter.
  (The letter was actually written Oct. 14th [**A.E.** 48, 87]).

I. Oct. 16th: Staupitz and Link, Luther's friends, agreed that the Cardinal would refuse to see Luther again, unless Luther would be willing to recant. The two left Augsburg that Saturday for Nuernberg traveling on two different roads.

J. Oct. 17th: Luther sent a message to the Cardinal that he would submit and remain silent, providing that the troubling indulgence peddler be disciplined.

K. Oct. 18th: Luther sent another message to the Cardinal that, since he was forbidden to see the Cardinal again without retracting, it was of no use for him to stay in Augsburg.

L. As Legate Cardinal Cajetan "maintained utter silence", Luther's friends, who were still in Augsburg, became uneasy. About midnight of October 20th to 21st Luther was secretly guided out of Augsburg. (The St. Anna Lutheran Church of Augsburg still displayed this whole episode with pictures in 1987.)

M. After narrow escape with his initial hard journey to Monheim, Luther arrived in Wittenberg October 31st. In his letter of appeal to Rome, which Luther had written on the 16th, he had included a "request for the retraction of the citation from Rome to the court from which he could expect no just decision."

N. In answer to Cajetan's letter to Frederick with quite brash instructions, the Elector expressed astonishment with a return letter that the Cardinal would make such outlandish request. When Luther was provided a copy of this letter, he was deeply encouraged and was led to truly rejoice. He finally was sure that the Elector would not hand him over to the power of Rome without a fair hearing on German soil.

O. In his written defense, submitted on the 14th, Luther exposed the various shams of papal claims, including that the pope claimed spiritual supremacy on earth, also over governments.

P. Luther now asked for a Free Christian Council. He insisted that the validity of a ban would have to depend on the decision of a Christian Council. He added this truth to his "Sermon on the Power of the Ban" that it was an honor for a Bible-based Christian to be put under a ban. (See Matthew 5:11-12; John 16:3-4; Acts 7:54-60 [all 3 passages refer to NIV]; et al.)

Q. In Wittenberg Luther also expanded his interpretation of the Lord's Prayer for the benefit of the common people.

R. He kept preaching: True instruction and knowledge of Christ happen when Christians understand that Christ is our true wisdom, righteousness, holiness, and redemption. Our own such assumptions are less than nothing. They are actually our folly, unrighteousness, and condemnation. (1. Cor. 1:30 [See NIV translation])

S. Luther's writings were in high demand everywhere and printers were reaping big profits.

T. While Luther was continuing his work in all his callings, he was also in a state of readiness to leave Wittenberg on very short notice.

U. On November 9th Rome declared the treasure of indulgences as official Roman doctrine. However, this newly reinforced declaration by Rome was not respected at all in Germany.

V. Luther was becoming ever more convinced from Scripture that the main teachings of the Roman Church were totally out of alignment with the main teachings of Scripture.

Questions about Chapter 14

1. (# A) Why was it in Luther's favor to receive a hearing in Augsburg rather than in Rome?

2. (# B) Why did previous reform-minded men not reach their goal? (Give two reasons.)

3. (# B) Why did Luther keep traveling to Augsburg, though many people advised against it?

4. (# C) Why did Luther not report to the cardinal right after his arrival?

5. (# D) What does the Latin word "R e v o c o" mean?

6. (#D,E,F,G) How many days did Luther and Cajetan actually meet face to face?

7. (#G) What did the Cardinal's absolute unwillingness to change his verdict tell us about his attitude toward Scripture?

8. (# H) Let's read from Luther's letter to Spalatin, who was a sort of mediator between Elector Frederick and Luther:

9. (# I) How did Link and Staupitz, Luther's friends, show that they did not trust Cajetan?

10. (# J) How did Luther, with his message to the cardinal on Oct. 17th, show that he could yield to some extend?

11. (# K & L) How many days did Martin Luther still stay in Augsburg after he had sent a second message to the Cardinal?

12. (# L) What seemed to be implied by the Cardinal's "maintaining (his) utter silence"?

13. (# M) What request had Luther registered with his letter to Rome on Oct. 16th?

14. (# N) What did Cajetan request of Elector Frederick that he do with Luther according to the Cardinal's letter of Oct. 23rd?

15. (# O) What two things astonished the Elector about the Cardinal's requests in respect to Luther and himself?

16. (# P) What effect did the Elector's letter to Cajetan have on Luther?

17. (# Q) What shams of Roman Catholicism had Luther exposed with his report (in Latin) late in 1518, wherewith he expressed direct opposition to papal supremacy?

18. (# R) Luther was now asking for a Free Christian Council. What did he want such a council to decide?

19. (# S) What other special writing and activity did Luther produce and continue during those days?

20. (# T) How were Luther's many writings being received at large?

21. (# U) How was Rome's declaration on Nov. 9, 1518, received in Germany, namely that the treasure of indulgences had been made Rome's official doctrine?

22. (# V) Of what did Luther now become ever more convinced?

VIII Chapters 15 - Miltitz with Outwardly Mitigated Tactics

Names and Places about Chapter 15

Urbanus von Serralonga — The pope's messenger who was supposed to lure Martin Luther to personally report to Cardinal Cajetan immediately after his arrival in Augsburg so that Cajetan could arrest Luther and send him directly to Rome. This plan was debunked.

Karl von Miltitz — The new softly-dealing legate from the pope to bring Luther to Rome, carrying lots of appeals to authorities in Germany for safe travel through their cities.

Archbishop Richard of Trier — Plan B: Miltitz wanted Luther to receive a hearing before this archbishop who was officiating in Trier, west of Frankfurt.

Summary of Chapter 15

A. Rome's previous plan was to deport Luther to Rome as quickly as possible.

B. Urbanus von Serralonga, a close friend of Cajetan, was a Roman nuncio, that is, a papal ambassador to a foreign country. It had been his assignment to lure Luther to report to Cardinal Cajetan as soon as possible after arriving in Augsburg, so that he could be arrested as a heretic and be sent to Rome. His friends had advised him strongly to first await documentation from Caesar Maximillian. Then he would be under Caesar's protective service. Luther did so and Rome's plan was debunked.

C. A new papal nuncio, Karl von Miltitz, came to pay a visit to Elector Frederick.

D. Some general information about the special rose, consecrated by the pope:

E. An explanation is provided, why Miltitz was supposed to ceremoniously present this rose to the Elector at just the right time.

F. Miltitz was also carrying special allowance letters, addressed to city councils in cities between Wittenberg and the Alps, for assistance to pass through with a prisoner.

G. Soon Miltitz found out that Luther's credit among Germans was quite a bit higher than the pope's credit.

H. Miltitz, aware that Caesar was terminally ill, wanted to meet with Luther as soon as possible. Elector Frederick approved such a hurried meeting to take place at Altenburg and instructed Luther accordingly. Luther went.

I. Miltitz treated Luther honorably, so different from what Cajetan's conduct had been.

J. Miltiz and Luther reached an agreement. Luther would stop writing and preaching against the church, providing that his opponents would do the same, all for peace in the church.

K. Luther's letter to the pope and his pamphlet to the people showed that he was still defending some false Roman teachings, but at the same time was also not letting go of a number of basic truths which he had learned from Holy Scripture.

L. Another letter of Luther to the pope showed his humble submission.

M. Miltitz hurried to set up a meeting for Luther with the Bishop of Trier as arbitrator.

N. Caesar Maximillian died at the beginning of spring, 1519. Now any agreement, which Miltiz had so masterfully arranged, was doomed for a number of reasons.

Questions about Chapter 15

1. (# A and B) What had been the plan of Rome through Cajetan at Augsburg?

2. (# B) How was that plan debunked?

3. (# I) Explain how Rome showed a completely reversed approach through Miltitz.

4. (# D) What was the consecrated rose?

5. (# E) What did the pope expect from the Elector for the favor of bestowing the consecrated rose on him?

6. (# F) What was the purpose of the special allowance letters Miltitz carried with him?

7. (# G) How much greater was Luther's credit than the pope's credit with the German people according to Miltitz's findings?

8. (# J, K, & L) What agreement did Miltitz and Luther reach?

9. (# M) Why was Miltitz in such a hurry to have Luther and the Bishop of Trier meet as soon as possible, with the bishop serving as arbitrator?

10. (# N) Why did the agreement between Miltitz and Luther have to fail?

IX Chapter 16 - The Debate at Leipzig - God Guided Luther to Begin Exposing Three Central False Teachings of Rome

Names and Places in Chapter 16

(the acclaimed pope) Sylvester — He was supposed to have received the big "Donation" from (314-335 A.D.) Emperor Constantine the Great during the 4th century

John Eck of Ingolstadt — Debater on behalf of Roman Catholicism, debated against Carlstadt in 1519 at Leipzig, and a couple days later against Luther

Summary of Chapter 16

A. Eck agreed to engage Carlstadt in public debate at Leipzig to defend his own "Obelisks".

B. However, Eck was actually attacking **Luther** with his pre-published theses about when the papacy began. Eck really had wanted to debate against Luther.

C. Luther requested of the Elector to be allowed to discontinue his promised silence.

D. Though Eck kept on not inviting Luther, he did keep on publicly accusing Luther of heresy.

E. Luther publicly answered Eck's public letter which had been attached to Eck's theses.

F. Luther wrote to Staupitz, informing him of two main hidden, but important, issues.

G. Duke George finally provided allowance for Luther to participate in the debate.

H. Name some of the causes which yielded high level excitement in Leipzig:

I. Eck requested on the 2nd day of the debate that the judges deny the use of books and notes, which was aimed against his opponent, Carlstadt. His request was granted.

J. About the phrase, "festival pericope" on p. 109: A pericope is a set of selected Sunday Scripture readings for the church year. This reference is to "the historic pericope". Main church festivals at that time of the year were: June 24th – the Nativity of John the Baptist; June 29th – the Festival of St. Peter & St. Paul; July 2nd – The Visitation (Mary visiting Elisabeth).

K. Luther was invited, but refused to enter the debate from July 1st – 3rd, because of biased governing rules. He finally did sign up to debate after it was granted that there would be no Roman judge on the panel for recording summaries of the debate.

L. Luther signed up on July 4th, the day John Tetzel died in a nearby monastery.

M. Luther attacked the pope's supreme power in the church. He did not yet attack the political power of the pope.

N. Note Luther's later comments about his defending the pope and not exposing him as the devil's tool.

O. Duke George's outcry, when Luther defended a part of the teachings of John Hus.

P. Luther kept insisting during following days that church councils can err, and that Scripture alone is infallible.

Q. Luther compared Eck's scanty knowledge of Scripture with a water spider.

R. Perhaps the debate might be properly assessed with the comments by Amsdorf as to who won the debate.

Questions about Chapter 16

1. (# A) Why did Dr. Eck choose the city of Leipzig for location of the debate?

2. Why had Luther remained silent in regard to participating in the debate?

3. (# B) Why was Luther stunned, when he saw the actual theses of Eck for the debate?

4. (# B) Why had Eck actually wanted to debate against Luther rather than against Carlstadt?

5. (# C) Why did Luther request of the Elector to let him reverse his promise of silence?

6. (# D) How did Eck publicly explain why he now regarded Luther as his enemy?

7. (# F) What were the 2 main points of which Luther informed Staupitz in his letter?

8. Why did Duke George move the debate from the Leipzig U to the Pleissen-Castle?

9. How had the public interpreted Carlstadt's accident as the Wittenberg contingent was entering Wittenberg?

10. (# H) Name some of the examples of the high-excitement level in Leipzig:

11. Why did Luther not want to have anything about the debate recorded?

12. Which two men were at the lecterns to begin the debate?

13. (# I) What debate procedure did Eck request of the judges to henceforth be denied on the 2nd day of the debate; and how was this aimed against Carlstadt?

14. (# J) Why did Luther use Matthew 16:13-19 as sermon text that weekend? Take notice of the two main points Luther made in his sermon?

15. How did the Leipzig doctors counter Luther's sermon on Matthew 16:13-19?

16. Why did it require a high degree of courage to preach as Luther had done that day?

17. What two things happened on the 4th of July?

18. Lets read paragraph 2 on p. 97:

19. (# O) Why was Duke George extremely upset, when Luther defended a teaching of John Hus?

20. (# P) What main positions did Luther keep holding all along in the debate?

21. (# Q) What was the meaning of the water spider applied to Eck in Luther's final speech?

22. On what date did the debate end?

23. What claims did Eck make for himself about the outcome of the debate?

24. How did Amsdorf refer to the whole debate in regard to who might have won?

X Chapters 17 - 18 - Luther Stays on Course

X Chapter 17 - Aftershocks of the Leipzig Debate

Names and Places in Chapter 17

Emser, Hieronymous — A Roman Catholic agitator among the students of Leipzig right before the Leipzig debate

Johann Oekolampad — A Swiss reformer, who entered the dispute as an anonymous writer at first, offering "The Planed-Down Eck" publication

New Battles

Bishop of Meissen — accused Luther of heresy in regard to the teaching of the Lord's Supper

Summary of Chapter 17

A. Luther stayed under attack
  1. Responding boastfully and wrongly, Eck claimed victory.
  2. Consequences for Luther were:
     a. He became favorably known in wider circles;
     b. the pope and Eck woke him up.
  3. Luther proceeded with writing explanations about his debate theses. He now kept insisting ever more firmly that Scripture is the only authority in matters of faith.
  4. Subsequent skirmishes:
     a. Eck's renewed accusations;
     b. Luther's fiery response;
     c. Eck's "Cleansing Publication";
     d. Luther's answer to the Bramardas (Screamer);
     e. An anonymous writer joined in the exchange of polemical writings with "The Planed-Down Eck".
  5. Emser entered the dispute as a trick writer. Luther unmasked him and described his claimed letter of praise as "The deed of a Joab against Abner" (See 2. Samuel 2-3 [consult NIV]) and "The Judas Kiss" (See Luke 22:47-48 [Consult NIV]).

Some Background Information:
John Hus (1369-1415) was born in Husenic, Bohemia. He became a priest in 1400. He was promoted to serve as rector (headmaster) of the U. of Prague in 1402, and also serve as preacher of the Bethlehem Chapel in Prague. After having been alerted to some of John Wycliffe's writings (via the Bohemian King Wenzel's sister, Anne of Luxemburg, who was married to Richard II in 1382 and was a promoter of Wycliffe's writings), he played a leading role in Prague toward reforming the corrupted church. In 1410 Wycliffe's books were burned by order of the church. In 1412 Huss was put under the ban by the church, because he kept professing Wycliffe's teachings. He published Wycliffe's teaching about the church, insisting that the Church is the body of the elect with Christ Jesus as its Head. He maintained that membership in the Roman Church is not automatically membership in God's Kingdom.

However, John Hus did not yet reject the teachings of transubstantiation, the intercession by saints, nor prayers for the dead. On July 6, 1415, after he had been accused and condemned as heretic by the Church Council of Kostnitz (or Costnitz, or Constance), Switzerland, and had been handed over to secular powers, he was burned alive, chained to a stake, even though he had been promised safe return to his home in Prague by Caesar Sigismund, by Pope Gregory XII (1406 ff.), Antipope Alexander V (1409 ff.), and the Antipope John XXIII (1410-1415). The rule which church leaders applied and requested of secular powers to be honored and applied was that no promise should be upheld against a person who has been declared a heretic.

    B. Polemical skirmishes developed into bigger battles.
        1. Eck and Emser accused Luther of the Hus heresy.
        2. By the end of 1519 Luther published, "A Sermon on the Highly Valued Sacrament of the Holy True Body of Christ." In this publication he set forth that both kinds in the Lord's Supper be distributed to lay members as well as to priests.
        3. Duke George showed himself as a big threat with his letter to Elector Frederick.
        4. Luther's clever short autobiography in answer to the accusation that he was a born Bohemian:
        5. Luther replied to Official Bishop of Meissen's denunciation of Luther. Luther answered with, "Dr. Martin's Reply to the Slips of Paper Which Were Issued under the Officil Seal of Stolpen."
        6. Miltitz and Duke George, regarding themselves well entertained, actually contributed toward putting out the new flare up against Luther by the Bishop of Meissen.
        7. Two western universities, Cologne and Lyon, condemned Luther, and Luther answered that they must use Scripture to substantiate their accusation, not scholastic quotations.
        8. Silvester Prierias issued a pamphlet, with which he defended the pope's so called primacy. Luther responded by tearing this publication apart and stating publicly that, if this were really Rome's position, then the pope truly must be the antichrist.

Questions about Chapter 17

1. (A, 1) How did Eck react after the debate?

2. (A, 2) In what way did Luther explain why the debate at Leipzig was good for him?

3. (A, 3) As Luther was writing up explanations about his theses in the debate at Leipzig, what main truth did he ever more strongly keep insisting must be accepted by all Christians?

4. (B, 1) Of what did Eck and Emser accuse Luther?

5. (B, 4) Why did Luther write a short autobiography?

6. (B, 6) How did Miltitz and Duke George help to extinguish the new attack against Luther which had been launched by the Bishop of Meissen?

7. (B, 7) With what advice did Luther answer the condemnation verdict of the universities of Cologne and Louvain?

8. (B, 8) Of what did the pamphlet of Prierias in regard to the pope's primacy persuade Luther? (Prierias was one of the pope's top advisers about Scripture doctrines.)

X Chapter 18 - Rome before the Court of the Christian Laity

Names and Places in Chapter 18

Augustine von Alveld — A Franciscan monk in Leipzig, who wanted to overpower Luther with his own dirty style of literacy

Archbishop Albrecht of Mainz — Bought nearly 8 bishop mantels from Rome, each costing 30,000 guilders

Lotter — A printer from Leipzig, who was persuaded to move to Wittenberg with a supply of German, Latin, and Greek letters, which current computer's "Office Microsoft" describes as "fonts"

Summary of Chapter 18

A. The Franciscan, Augustine von Alveld of Leipzig, wrote against Luther in line with papal claims, and Luther answered with, "From Popedom in Rome against the Very Famous Roman in Leipzig," in respect to the basic question: has the papacy been established by divine order, or by human order.

B. Luther exposed Alveld's false claims with three points:
1. His foul language;
2. His false use of reason about the pope and the Church;
3. That the O.T. was a preview of the N.T.

C. Finally Luther advised what Alveldt should really do.

D. Luther's clear explanation of Matthew 18:18 and John 21:22-23 in conjunction with Matthew 16:19 "I will give you the keys of the kingdom of heaven."

E. Luther's opinion why God allowed the pope to keep doing damage, and what his own position was in regard to the power of Rome.

F. The author, Graebner, recognized three things about Luther's changing position and proceeded to show why Luther had turned to target the laity as his audience.

G. Luther had "amazing energy", as he relentlessly kept applying himself for the cause of the gospel, including his writing of pamphlets and monitoring their distribution.

H. At the same time Luther kept being relentlessly occupied in his work at the U of Wittenberg.

I. Luther now decided to target the German nobility with his writings.

Questions about Chapter 18

1. (B) Augustine von Alveldt claimed that every earthly organization must have a head. Hence, he identified the pope as the head of the church. What did Luther show was wrong with Alveldt's assumptions?

2. How did Luther explain Christ's identifying his Church?

3. To whom did Christ give the power to forgive and retain sin?

4. According to Luther's words why did God allow the papal power to continue on earth? Note how Luther's words agree with the prophecy through the Apostle Paul in 2. Thessalonians 2:3-4 and 9-12.

5. (F) Let's read the bottom paragraph on p. 128 to note the three things which the author of the book recognized about Luther's position at that point in his life.

6. To whom does the expression, the Laity, refer?

7. (I) Besides instructing people at large with his preaching and pamphlets, and besides actively training next generation pastors with God's Word at the U of Wittenberg, to what other group would Luther now turn with the hope of reformation of the corrupted church?

XI Chapter 19 - Luther Addressing the German Nobility

Names and Places in Chapter 19

Teutleben, Valentin — An adviser in Rome, who warned Elector Frederick that Luther could become a big problem for him. The Elector handled that advise well.

Ulrich von Hutten — A noble knight, who stood with Luther in battle against the pope

Franz von Sickingen — Another noble night, but also a humanist, who offered shelter to Luther, should Luther have to move out of Wittenberg

Summary of Chapter 19

A. The German economy was being targeted damagingly because of the political oppression by the Roman church, which claimed to have higher authority than any secular power.

B. As Luther's life was regarded in great danger after the Leipzig debate, some nobles offered him protective refuge, should Wittenberg become unreliable.

C. However, Elector Frederick kept protecting Luther. He wanted Luther to be given the right to defend his teachings before competent judges and on German soil.

D. In his relationship with the Elector Luther did want to retain full rights to function in his office.

E. Hutten did inform Luther about L. Valla's writing about the "Constantine Donation" fraud.

F. Instead of hiding among the nobles for protection Luther wanted to elevate the nobility.

G. The title of Luther's address to the nobility: "To the Christian Nobility of the German Nation about Improvement for Existing Christian Conditions."

H. In his letter to Amsdorf on June 23, 1520, Luther included the statement that he now would play the role of court jester within the framework of the nobility.

I. Luther began, urging the nobility not to put their trust in their own power and reason, rather to despair due to their lack of strength, humbly trust in God, and seek his help.

J. Luther described the three walls, which the Roman church had erected around itself.

K. He next reviewed regarding what was commonly understood under spiritual professions and under secular professions, but then described the real spiritual body.

L. Correct the functions of high rank church office holders and the first wall would be gone.

M. The second wall also would tumble, when Christians align church office descriptions with what Holy Scripture teaches, instead of allowing high rank office holders to decide these.

N. The third wall, that only popes can issue summons for councils, then falls by itself.

O. No Christian is allowed to damage the truth but only to promote the truth. (2. Cor. 13:8)

P. Luther next exposed and denounced the Roman church's rank system and its worldly greed, as was recognized by its assuming ownership and full control of land and real estate.

Q. The main reason Rome gave for conducting indulgence sales and other fund raising programs.

R. Some of the 26 areas, which Luther cited as being in need of reform:

    a. Monasteries and Orders

    b. Salary support for pastors,

    c. Festivals and certain masses,

d. Penances with their penal codes,

   e. Fasting and various food restrictions,

   f. Different letters for indulgences, butter and foods, masses, etc.

   g. Different alignments in universities, also for lower schools,

   h. About the use of books and the rating of schools.

S. This writing of Luther was excitedly received in wider circles but hit like a bomb in Rome.

T. A papal bull was under way to be later followed by the ban.

Questions about Chapter 19

1. (# E) Name two members of the German nobility who got their portrait into the Luther biography.

2. (# E) **Point of information** regarding the claimed "Donation of Constantine" mentioned on p. 135:
   Under Rome's own admission (Catholic Encyclopedia V, p. 118) "The Donation of Constantine" is a "forged document of Emperor Constantine the Great (272-370) to the acclaimed Pope Sylvester I (314-335) by which large privileges and rich possessions were said to have been conferred on the Pope of the Roman Church." (From the pamphlet: "The Split between Roman Catholicism and Christ" p. 8).

3. (# B) Why did some nobles offer their castles to Luther as havens of refuge? What had they been thinking might happen?

4. What motivated Elector Frederick to protect Luther against the papacy?

5. (# H) What role was Luther ready to play among the nobles according to his letter to Amsdorf?

6. (# I) How did Luther advise the nobles to proceed, as they might undertake reformation in the empire?

7. (# J) Identify the three walls for preserving church power which the Roman church had erected around itself.

8. (# K) What basic truth did Luther set forth with his example scenario?

9. (# M) What would take down the second self-protecting wall of the Roman church?

10. (# O) Quote the Bible passage with which Luther supported the truth which the previous question set forth:

11. About how much money was estimated that Rome was getting out of Germany annually to support their church operation? Does 40 million dollars sound shocking?

12. (# Q) Can you recall what two main purposes Rome claimed, in order to be served with the proceeds from indulgence sales and other money raising gimmicks?

13. (# R.) What mistake might be regarded as common to all eight points that needed reform under Luther's cited list of "26 spiritual improprieties"?

14. What impression would you feel Luther's address to the nobility would have given to the nobility?

   to the common people?

   to the clergy, to Rome?

15. When does a church officer's ranking system become un-Christian and even abusive?

XII Chapter 20 - The Papal Banning Bull

Names and Places in Chapter 20

Aleander	- A baptized Jew, who worked side by side with the other Dr. Eck in Rome, both of them staunch enemies of Luther
Cardinal Accolti	- Drew up the wording of the papal banning bull against Luther
Cardinal de Vio	- Assistant in the drawing up of the banning bull
Carlstadt, Feldkirchen, Adelmann, Pirkheimer, and Spengler	- All these were also named as co-conspirators with Luther and were included under the papal ban.
Muehlpfort, Hieronymous	- Mayor of Zwickau to whom Luther dedicated the German edition of his treatise, "About the Freedom of a Christian"

Summary of Chapter 20

Having addressed the German nobility with a powerful writing, Luther let three more powerful writings be printed about the same time the papal bull against him was being delivered.

The meaning of three expressions: **Papal Bull** – a special decree or declaration from the pope; **Ban (during Luther's life time)** – an official document with which a persistent false teacher, many times including his followers, was deprived of all spiritual rights, even his earthly possessions, and many times was also condemned to death; **Interdict** – a complete refusal of forgiveness of sins and most, if not all, spiritual benefits from a ruler, a city, and sometimes a whole country, in answer to persistent opposition to the pope.

A. The drafting and plans for enforcing the papal bull against Luther.
   1. Having been authorized to deliver the bull, Eck was allowed to add several other names besides Luther's.
   2. Some cities allowed the posting of the bull, others didn't.
   3. Travelling back home from having attended the coronation at Aachen, the Elector was handed a copy of the banning bull. He was deeply upset for several reasons.
   4. Luther showed himself quite calm about all of it.
   5. Miltitz kept holding on to his role as mediator and with support of several influential Augustinians advised Luther to write a letter to the pope, explaining that he had not been attacking the pope in person.

B. About **"The Babylonian Captivity of the Church"**
   1. Luther was showing himself to be much firmer than he had been 2 years earlier. He wrote a tract against the main abomination of the papacy with "Sermon of the New Testament, i.e., about the Holy Mass."
   2. The papacy was holding the Church, the body of believers, captive with the falsified celebration of the Lord's Supper:
      a. Giving only one kind to the laity was contrary to Christ's command.
      b. Having imposed a false transubstantiation interpretation, they also included the false teaching that the earthly elements are supposed to no longer be present after the words of consecration have been spoken.
      c. Claiming that Christ's body and blood are re-sacrificed regularly in the mass.
   3. Luther also showed that there are only two Sacraments, not 7, like Rome was claiming.
   4. Yet, Luther still wanted to resolve false issues in the church in friendly manner.

C. The pamphlet **"About the Freedom of a Christian"**
  1. Luther's very friendly letter to the pope was attached to this pamphlet. Luther dedicated the German issue of this pamphlet to the mayor of Zwickau, Hieronymous Muehlpfort.
  2. Summary of the first part of the pamphlet
     a. "A look at the internal man"
     b. God's Word produces the Christian by applying both law and gospel. This happens only by faith.
     c. This leads to the understanding of what Good works really are.
     d. This pamphlet, together with the accompanying letter to the pope, shows in Luther's conclusion that he really had remained friendly toward the pope.
D. Immediately after Luther had received the bull and was convinced that the bull actually had been issued by the pope, did he answer with the writing, **"Against the Bull of the Antichrist"**.
  1. In this document he now showed himself free in relation to the pope and his bull.
  2. He stepped forth, pointing at the pope as the real Scripturally foretold Antichrist.
E. The Elstergate Bonfire message
F. Luther published a declaration in both German and Latin, "Why the Books of the Pope and His Disciples Are Burned: Let It Be Shown by Anyone, Why They Have Burned the Books of Dr. Luther."
G. Luther retracted parts of his original 95 Theses.
H. How the papal ban was commanded by the pope to be applied to all of Luther's followers as well as to Luther in person.
I. Luther had also been asked, by the Elector and others, to issue a public writing against the Roman Banning Bull. Luther did so with the publication, "Reason and Cause of All the Articles Which Were Unjustly Condemned by the Roman Bull."

Questions about Chapter 20

1. What was the title of the new leader of the Holy Roman Empire? Last line of chapter 20 and first 9 lines of chapter 21.

2. (A – 1) Name at least two instigators who requested that Luther be put under the papal bull.

3. (A – 3) Why did the Elector become very upset?

4. Can you recall from O.T. history the name of the country into which Israel was taken to be their slaves? See 2. Kings 25:1-21 for a graphic description of that massive deportation.

5. (B) How did Luther incorporate that historic story into the title of one of his special writings in 1520?

6. (B – 2) What three heresies had the papal power forced on the Christian Church about the celebration of the Lord's Supper?

7. Why did Luther reduce the number of sacraments from 7 to 2 (for a little while from 7 to 3)?

8. (C – 2 – d) How was Luther inclined toward the pope when he wrote the pamphlet, "About the Freedom of a Christian"?

9. What two *seeming* contradictory statements of the Bible did Dr. Luther expound under the title, "About the Freedom of a Christian"?

10. (C – 2 – c) With what examples did Luther describe believing Christian as doers of good works?

11. (D) Once Luther was convinced that it was really the pope who issued the bull against him, with what document did he respond?

12. (G) Why did Luther retract parts of his original 95 Theses?

13. On whom did the pope declare an interdict with his papal bull against the so called Lutheran heresy?

14. What additional penalties did the pope decree with his bull against Luther?

15. (E) What event did Luther sponsor at the Elstergate of the Augustinian monastery in answer to the previously universally proclaimed burning of Luther's books?

XIII Chapter 21 - Testifying before the Imperial Diet at Worms

Names and Places in Chapter 21

Karl V	- Caesar of the Holy Roman Empire, succeeding Maximilian
Wilhelm von Croix	- The Secretary of State of the empire
Glapio	- The Franciscan father confessor for Caesar Karl V
Ziska	- A wild leader of the Hussites in the war of the empire against the Bohemians about 100 years before the German Reformation
Ambrosius Katharinus	- A Roman theologian who wrote a book, warning against the Lutheran teachings, to which Luther responded with a Latin essay
Lucas Cranach	- An artist who produced quite a few portraits for reformation history
Duke George	- A bitter enemy of Luther until 1539, residing in the Leipzig area
Kaspar Sturm	- A royal herald who provided safe escort for Luther to and from Worms
Amsdorf	- A Wittenberg professor, who accompanied Luther to Worms
Ferdinand	- He had married his cousin, Queen Isabella. Together they had led rescue operation against Islam invasion in Spain. They were the grandparents of Carl V. Carl's brother was also named Ferdinand.
Duke Erich von Braunschweig	- offered Luther a drink of beer as he left the imperial court
Hans von Minkwitz	- A knight who was ill, to whom Luther administered private Communion before leaving Worms
Albrecht Duerer	- An artist who mourned Luther's sudden disappearance
Schurf and Justus Jonas	- co-travelers of Luther to Wittenberg
Hieronymous Vehus	- Negotiator for Rome after the imperial session, trying to get Luther to reverse his position
King Christian II of Denmark	- Bargained for Luther after the sessions

Summary of Chapter 21

A. Huge complications in preparation for Caesar's first imperial diet had to be taken into account.
  1. The coronation of Charles V as Caesar of the Holy Roman Empire took place in Aachen, Germany, on October 23, 1520.
  2. Luther's appeal to Caesar for a fair hearing of the truth was not answered. Spalatin thought that support from the new Caesar looked very slim, at best. This early assessment actually caused Luther to rejoice, because in this way Psalm 118:9 (NIV) would teach his flock the important lesson of putting their trust in God above trust in worldly power.
  3. Turmoil was brewing in the empire due to the excessive demands by the papal regime. It was feared that it could grow into rebellion against Rome.
  4. It took some time for government authorities to reach a decision, whether or not to summon the Augustinian monk, Luther, to the diet for purpose of testifying in response to the papal banning bull against him. Elector Frederick of Saxony had maintained his position that Luther be given a fair hearing in Germany.

      5. Luther assured the Elector that he definitely would attend the diet at Worms, should he be summoned.
- B. 37 days after the opening of the diet they reached a decision to summon Luther.
  1. While the diet was in session since January 28th, Luther kept actively pursuing his ministry in Wittenberg.
  2. Legate Aleander had delivered an excessively long speech and had been actively bribing against Luther, along with political ploys by other Romanists.
  3. As German nobles and Rome's representatives were parleying back and forth, the nobles putting forth 101 German grievances against Roman renewed demands, the Diet participants actually reached agreement to extend a quite amicable invitation to Luther on March 6th.
- C. Luther's trip to Worms lasted 15 days:
  1. The royal herald, Kaspar Sturm, arrived in Wittenberg March 26th, with Caesar's promise of save escort. Luther left Wittenberg April 2nd.
  2. A last ditch effort by Glapio, one of Caesar's counselors, to divert Luther, along with some other scary tactics failed to cause Luther to go back home.
  3. Luther arrived in Worms on Tuesday, April 16th.
- D. Luther before Caesar and the empire
  1. After two hours of waiting on April 17th, 1521, Luther was admitted into the Diet hall before Caesar, his brother, Ferdinand, six electors, and about 200 high lords.
  2. He was confronted with a twofold question by the hereditary marshal:
     a. Are these your books? and
     b. Will you retract them or defend them?
  3. Luther's answer:
     a. Yes!
     b. I need time to think about this second question that I shall answer without prejudice toward God's Word and toward my soul.
  4. Luther was given one day so that he could answer the question properly.
  5. The next day Luther gave his answer that he could not retract any of his books.
  6. Caesar gave his harsh verdict the next day, April 19th.
- E. The conclusion at Worms and Luther's homeward journey
  1. Caesar yielded to the nobles to continue correspondence with Luther till April 24th.
  2. Luther kept insisting that he must be bested with Holy Scripture, not by way of decretals and scholastic logic in order to retract.
  3. Caesar extended Luther's time at Worms another two days, to April 26th. But on the 25th Luther asked to be allowed to go back home. This was granted.
  4. Safe escort for 21 days was reaffirmed. Luther left Worms April 26th in quietness.
  5. Unexpectedly the surprising news came that Luther had been attacked. No one seemed to know who the attacker(s) was or, whether Luther even had been killed.
  6. Caesar signed an edict against Luther on May 26th, giving him the title of heretic, condemned by the pope. The four remaining electors also signed the edict, retroactively dated to May 8, 1520, as though it was the unanimous decision by all six electors.

Questions about Chapter 21

1. (A - 2) We would feel stronger, if the supreme court were convinced that aborting unborn children is equivalent to murder. Why was Luther happy, when Charles V. would not give support to Luther's appeal for support of the truth, but allowed Luther's books to be burned at Cologne?

2. (A - 3) If large segments of people decide to proceed toward open rebellion for the sake of the truth, why should we not participate?

3. For what two reasons did Elector Frederick want to stay neutral regarding Luther's cause?

4. What influenced Caesar Charles V so much to react by recommending safe escort for Luther to and from Worms?

5. What political scheme did Caesar's counselor, Glapio, employ to divert Luther from coming to Worms?

6. (C – 3) How many days did it take Luther to reach Worms?

7. What other special ploy did counselor Glapio attempt to sidetrack Luther from going all the way to Worms and report to the diet?

8. (D – 2) What two questions were asked of Luther to answer before the whole assembly of the diet?

9. (D – 3) What was Luther's answer on his first day, April 17th, before the diet assembly?

10. Let's read Luther's response to the basically same question on the second day as he was testifying before the whole assembly of the diet.

11. What was Caesar Charles V's verdict concerning Luther the day after Luther had testified?

12. (E – 1 & 3) When Caesar was persuaded to extend correspondence with Luther, how many days in all was this correspondence carried on?

13. (E - 4) How did Luther's departure from Worms differ significantly from his arrival 11 days earlier?

14. (E - 5) What was the surprise ending of the whole episode at Worms?

15. (E – 6) To what illegal document did Caesar affix his signature on May 26th?

16. (E – 6) Why was this actually an illegal edict?

XIV Chapters 22 - 23 - While Luther Was Being Kept in Seclusion, Destruction of the Reformation Went into Motion

XIV Chapter 22 - Patmos

Names and Places in Chapter 22

Hans von Borlepsch	- Knight and captain of the Wartburg
Burkhard Hund	- Fellow friendly kidnapper of Luther on his way home
Squire George	- Luther's new name at the Wartburg
Latomus	- A theologian at the U. of Lyon, who wrote against Luther, which Luther answered straight out of the Bible, not having access to any other background scholastic writings at that time

Summary of Chapter 22

A. "Patmos", the name of the island where the Apostle John was held "because of the Word of God and the testimony of Jesus," (Rev. 1:9 [NIV]) was applied by Luther, while he was being hidden at the Wartburg. This 10 months friendly incarceration of Luther, as he was kept at the Wartburg away from Wittenberg, seemed to fit, while Rome was still wanting to get their hands on him.

B. Luther traveled homeward through Friedberg, Hersfeld, Berka, Eisenach, Moehra.

C. During the beginning of May the friendly kidnapping was executed by Berlepsch and Hund. Luther was taken to the Wartburg.

D. While at the Wartburg, Luther was occupied with letter writing and even participated in a hunt in his own way.

E. He finished interpreting the Magnificat and several Psalms, but still could not entirely shake off some of his old papal mindsets.

F. His new identity was "Squire George". He also occupied himself with writing the Postil.

G. Using only the Bible as resource, he wrote a refutation against Latomus of Lyon.

H. He sent his critique of the pope's Lord's Supper Bull to the pope.

I. He undertook his most important work at the Wartburg, translating the N.T. This translation he finished in 11 weeks.

J. Note the description of the sort of language he used for translating the N.T.

K. The Archbishop Albrecht started resuming his old money raising scheme by offering the display of his large collection of relics in Halle. A few of these relics are described.

L. Luther let Wittenberg know how he was going to respond to Albrecht's relics display. He also did not refrain from opposing the Elector's non-toleration warning.

M. The archbishop responded. He actually reversed his plans completely. This included pardoning the priest who had dared to get married and therefore had been incarcerated.

Questions about Chapter 22

1. (B) Why may it have been special for Luther to visit Moehra and Eisenach?

2. (A) Who had arranged for the kidnapping of Luther, and why?

3. (D,E,F,G) Can you name at least three different writings of Luther while he was at the Wartburg?

4. (I) What was Luther's most important work while he was at the Wartburg?

5. Lets read the last paragraph on p. 187:

6. (K) What special project did Archbishop Albrecht again resume in Halle?

7. How did Luther overtrump the Elector's non-toleration forbiddance in regard to attacking the Archbishop of Mainz?

8. What two main wrongs did Luther request the archbishop to correct?

9. With what action did Luther threaten the archbishop, if he would not stop and/or reverse his idolatrous activity at that time?

10. (M) What was accomplished with Luther's threatening letter to the archbishop?

XIV Chapter 23 Disruptions at Wittenberg

Names and Places in Chapter 23

Johann Bugenhagen	- Main preacher in the city church at Wittenberg
Gabriel Zwilling	- Another preacher, who along with Carlstadt wanted to advance reformation their own way and in the process they were increasing turmoil in Wittenberg and moving in the direction of rebellion.
Storch and Stuebner	- The false fire and brimstone prophets of Zwickau, who were preaching rebellion, claiming that God was communicating his messages to them directly with visions and dreams
Thomas Muenzer	- also had been preaching disorderliness in Zwickau in the same fashion as Storch and Stuebner
Nicolaus Hausmann	- Pastor at Zwickau, who challenged the false preachers to defend themselves before the city council, whereupon the false teachers left the area

Summary of Chapter 23

A. In Wittenberg things actually looked good at first with Luther out of the way.

B. Carlstadt decided to return from Denmark and continue his work of the reformation at Wittenberg. He set up theses for debate, aimed toward revolution.

C. Luther heard about the resulting confusion and wrote "About Monastic Vows", attempting to dissuade the participating monks from changing their life styles and forcing the whole issue too soon.

D. Two commissions were set up in the University of Wittenberg. Both ended up with divided conclusions. However, now Melanchthon began to voice his objection in regard to the new movement.

E. Luther issued another pamphlet about "The Misuse of the Masses", but the rebellious movement just kept spreading.

F. During the same month, December, when Luther proceeded to translate the N.T. into German, he also paid a secret visit to some of the faculty in Wittenberg.

G. Luther expressed two concerns in a letter to Amsdorf. Because the people had gone too far, Luther issued another writing, namely, "A True Admonition to All Christians to Watch Themselves against Insurrection and Rebellion."

H. Carlstadt kept his ball rolling with year-end official changes, increasing the disruptions.

I. Besides Carlstadt, four additional disrupting preachers were identified as false prophets in action: Zwilling, Stuebner, Storch, and Muenzer.

J. Melanchthon just did not know how to properly assess and correct these false prophets. The Elector also was at a loss, except that he did not want to see quick changes in the officiating within churches.

K. Note the translator's comments, why translating the word "Schwaermer" with "swarmers" may be more accurate and to the point than the expression, "religious enthusiasts".

L. Only Luther appeared to be able to assess the problem at the bottom of the disruptions in Wittenberg.

M. The reformation movement in Wittenberg appeared to be falling apart.

N. Luther decided to come out of hiding despite the elector's strong objection.

O. Luther was rebuking the Elector as he was leaving the Wartburg on March 1, 1522, after 10 months of protective incarceration.

Questions about Chapter 23

1. (B) Why did Carlstadt cut his visit to Denmark short according to Graebner?

2. (B) What was wrong with Carlstadt's interpretation of 1. Timothy 3:2 (NIV)?

3. (D & E) What was the main problem for the two commissions which were set up?

4. (F) Why did Luther pay a secret visit to Wittenberg?

5. (G) What two concerns did Luther express in his letter to Amsdorf?

6. (G) Give one main point in Luther's pamphlet "To All Christians against Insurrection and Rebellion."

7. (H) Name a couple of Carlstadt's premature requirements for his kind of reformation.

8. (I) Name three of the five disruptive agents, who had become active at that time.

9. (J) Why couldn't Melanchthon and the Elector distinguish correctly and take proper action in response to the false prophets?

10. (N) Why would Luther no longer obey the Elector, as he decided to come out of hiding?

11. (O) For what action did Luther rebuke the Elector while he was coming out of the hiding at the Wartburg?

XV Chapters 24 - 25 - The Reformation Work Is Resumed

XV Chapter 24 - The Smothering of the Disruptions at Wittenberg

Names and Places in Chapter 24

Storch and Stuebner   - See under chapter 23
Y.E.G.   - Abbreviation for addressing: Your Electoral Grace

Summary of Chapter 24

A. Meet the mystery man at the Bear's Inn outside of Jena.
B. Luther's answer to his YEG, (**Y**our **E**lectoral **G**race).
C. Luther also satisfied the Elector's precautionary request.
D. Luther appeared in healthier outward appearance in the pulpit for eight days in a row.
E. Zwilling repented and continued with Luther. Carlstadt remained deceptive and receded.
F. Luther dealt with the Zwickau false prophets, Stuebner and Storch.
G. Luther's treatise about, "Receiving the Sacrament in Both Kinds and Other Renewals", and his epistle to Kronberg; Note:
   1. Luther's directive to those who were claiming false religious neutrality; and,
   2. His comment in connection with Germanizing the Bible.
H. Luther also found time to preach at Borna, Altenburg, Zwickau, and Eilenburg. About 25,000 heard him preach at Zwickau.
I. Luther also did go to Erfurt to preach the Word, which dampens rebellious activity.
J. Shrovetide: Three days before going to Confession prior to Ash Wedesday; 3 days before Lent.

Questions about Chapter 24

1. (A) Who was the mystery man, and what was he doing in the Bear's Inn?

2. (B) What did Luther write to the Elector in reference to Duke George?

3. (B) Why was the Elector so careful in respect to Duke George?

4. (F) Who were the Zwickau prophets, and what were they preaching?

5. (F) How did Luther request of Stuebner and also of Storch to prove their divine calling for their claimed revised reformation policy? (See Deut. 18:20-22 [NIV] and 13:1-5 [NIV])

6. (G - 1) How did Luther counsel those who were laying claim to a false religious neutrality?

7. Why couldn't Luther go after the swarming false prophets in other localities right away?

8. What had produced rebellious reformation at Erfurt?

9. How did Luther help out toward subduing the rebellious activity at Erfurt?

XV Chapter 25 - Planting and Watering

Names and Places in Chapter 25

Cranach — An artist who did a number of the paintings, sketches and woodcuts, which are used as illustrations in the book

Bugenhagen — The pastor of the city church in Wittenberg

Summary of Chapter 25

A. A new beginning with the translation of the New Testament into German, Sept. 21, 1522:

B. The begrudging response of opponents, including Duke George, and Emser's plagiarism:

C. Spiritually enlightened people actively confessed the message of Holy Scripture.

D. Luther pressed on, translating books of the O. T. and preaching and teaching daily.

E. The enlarged Church Postil was now being supplied for the festival half of the church year.

F. More preachers were being trained at the U. of Wittenberg. Ever more papal sour dough was being swept out. Luther insisted that Scripture readings must be in the people's language.

G. The story of the first Lutheran hymnal and its effect.

H. Luther's urging, "To the Mayors and Councils of All Cities in Germany That They Erect and Maintain Christian Schools." He decried all schools that don't teach Holy Scripture and warned that the Word will pass on **like a rain shower**. (Make the most of it while it's here.

I. The teaching of languages was regarded as being very important. Congregations were not yet fully developed like we know them today.

Questions about Chapter 25

1. Where had Luther translated the New Testament of Holy Scripture?

2. How was this printed translation received in cities where the Roman Catholic Church was in control?

3. (C) How did the common people in Saxony receive this translation?

4. How far had Luther and his co-workers advanced in translating the O. T. by the beginning months of 1523?

5. (E) With what book did Luther help preachers who didn't really know how to preach, or even just to write a proper sermon?

6. (F) What was some of the "papal sour dough" in teaching and practice, that kept being swept out, issue by issue?

7. (G) Name two of Luther's hymns which were included in the first Lutheran hymnal, that consisted of 8 hymns in all?

8. (H) What did Luther urge mayors and city councils to promote as urgent business?

9. (I) What did Luther describe as a good school, and what did he regard as a bad school?

10. Why didn't it work out to manage a congregation with a parochial school at Leisnig on the Mulde River?

XVI Chapters 26 - 28 - God's Word Applied to More Serious National Disruptions

XVI Chapter 26 - Luther's Counsel for High and Low

Names and Places in Chapter 26

Y.R.D.	- Abbreviation for addressing Duke George as "**Y**our **R**oyal **D**isgrace" as Luther answered Duke George's question to him, whether Luther had written the letter to Hartmuth von Kronberg, which Duke George regarded as very insulting to himself
Hadrian VI (1522-1523)	- The newly elected pope after Leo X
Clemens VII (1523-1533)	- The pope in Rome after the short reign of Hadrian VI

Summary of Chapter 26

A. Luther eased troubled consciences:
   1. For people at large with special writings and pamphlets;
   2. For troubled nuns, helping them to escape, and writing on their behalf;
   3. For monks wanting to get out of monastic sinfulness and get married;
   4. For soldiers in the imperial army as they took note of Luther's truthfulness and persistence for the cause of the reformation.

B. Luther's un-apologetic answer to Duke George, who had become very upset about Luther's letter to Hartmuth von Kronberg (the spelling of "Kronberg" kept being juggled).

C. Luther responded to professionals, national leaders, who make decisions at diets.
   1. 1522, the new pope, Hadrian VI, was determined to deal with the case of Luther.
   2. The professionals requested a Christian Council on German soil.
   3. The humanist supportive knights, Sickingen and Hutten, were killed in battle.
   4. 1523, another pope, Clemens VII, took office after Hadrian VI had died.
   5. Luther responded to contradicting resolutions by two diets (empire conventions at Worms and Nuernberg) with the writing, "Two Imperial Disagreeing and Contradicting Commands against Luther."
      a. Counseling, "Something eerie needs to be realized."
      b. Reminding that only God will decide the date for Luther's death.
   6. Legate Campeggi conducted a semi-secret conference to get more support for executing the Edict of Worms.

Questions about Chapter 26

1. (A – 1) What counsel did Luther provide for common people? Name at least two of his writings.

2. (A – 2) How did Luther help troubled nuns?

3. (A – 3) How did Luther ease troubled consciences of monks for whom monastic living had become too big of a struggle?

4. (A – 4) How did Luther's persistence for the cause of the reformation affect some of the soldiers in the imperial army?

5. What did Luther think about some clergy beginning to get married?

6. (B) What wording in Luther's letter to Kronberg deeply upset Duke George?

7. (C – 5) Luther counsels the lordships of two separate diets, Worms and Nuernberg, for adopting contradictory resolutions. What is the name of Luther's writing with which he responded to such sloppy legislating?

8. (C – 3) What happened to the two leaders among the knights, Sickingen and Hutten?

9. (C – 6) What semi-secret campaign did legate Cambeggi set into motion?

XVI Chapter 27 - Confronting the Allstedt Spirit

Names and Places in Chapter 27

Cranach and Bugenhagen   - See chapter 25

Summary of Chapter 27

A. Carlstadt got himself elected by way of disorderly procedure as pastor of Orlamuende.
  1. He started writing against Wittenberg.
  2. Four of Csrldtsdt's reformation revisions included:
     a. Instituting the Jewish Sabbath;
     b. Setting up a stronger ban and interdict than that of the Roman Church;
     c. Doing away with baptism;
     d. Writing against the real presence of the Lord's body and blood in the Lord's Supper.
B. Even worse, Muenzer of Allstedt began preaching outright and violent rebellion.
  1. Luther advised the 2 Saxon counts, Elector and Johann. The Allstedt spirit is very evil.
  2. Luther confronted Carlstadt at the dining table at Jena and invited him to debate against him at Wittenberg, and Carlstadt accepted.
  3. Two clear illustrations at Kahla and Jena exposed the Allstedt spirit for Luther.
C. Luther issued a special writing about the swarmers, namely, "Against the Heavenly Prophets about Pictures and the Sacrament."

Questions about Chapter 27

1. (A) How did Carlstadt become pastor at Orlamuende?

2. What was disorderly about Carlstadt's becoming preacher of Orlamuende?

3. (A – 2) Name several false teachings of Carlstadt!

4. (B) How was Muenzer's procedure even worse than Carlstadt's procedure?

5. (B – 1) How did Luther counsel the two Saxon counts with his assessment of the swarmers?

6. (B – 2) Why did Luther give Carlstadt a gold guilder at Jena?

7. How did Luther recognize the Allstedt spirit at Kahla and at Jena?

8. (C) After Carlstadt was ordered out of the country, what special writing did Luther have printed against Carlstadt and his company?

9. What did Luther anticipate would happen after the Allstedt spirit would be set into motion?

Brief distinction between the three Fredericks:
>Frederick the Wise, Elector of Saxony (1486-1525)

>Elector John Frederick of Saxony, or Frederick the Constant
>(Brother of Frederick the Wise) (1525-1532)

>Elector John Frederick the Magnanimous (Son of Frederick the Constant, 1532-1547)

XVI Chapter 28 - Opposing the Peasant War
Names and Places in Chapter 28

Carlstadt   - See chapter 8
Muenzer   - See chapter 23

Summary of Chapter 28

A. The rebellion had started.
    1. Luther wrote a forewarning, applying it to higher authorities as well as to farmers.
    2. Strong skirmishes began in the Black Forest area.
    3. Muenzer returned to Thuringia and preached rebellion without mercy for opponents. *
B. While helping out at Eisleben Luther wrote, "Admonition toward Peace in regard to the Twelve Articles of the Farmers' Alliance in Swabia."
C. When the rebellion spread into Thuringia, Luther went into the middle of it, preaching against it. He soon found out that there was no way of stopping it.
D. Luther next issued a new publication, "Against the Murdering and Robbing Rabble of Farmers."
E. The rebellion was subdued forcefully. Muenzer and Pfeifer were executed as rebellion leaders.
F. May 5, 1525, Elector Frederick the Wise fell asleep. Luther was called home to preach for the funeral.
G. Both sides of the peasant war blamed Luther for it. Luther responded with the "Epistle about the Harsh Pamphlet against the Farmers."
H. Carlstadt came to Luther asking for help. Luther interceded for him and saved him from being executed. Carlstadt promised to stop preaching and settle as a quiet village resident.

Questions about Chapter 28

1. (A - 2) Where did rebellion begin to break out?

2. (A – 3) Take a good look at that rebellion. Note how devastating it is. (Read the last paragraph on p. 231)

3. (B) How did Luther answer the indirect invitation from Swabia's 12 Articles for purpose of joining the rebellion movement?

4. (C) What special effort did Luther make to try and stop the rebellion, when it had advanced into Thuringia?

5. (D) What new writing did Luther then issue?

6. (E, H) How did the rebellion end for Muenzer, for Pfeifer, for Carlstadt?

7. (G) How did things turn out for Luther after the suppression of the revolt?

8. (F) What other special event took place in the midst of the peasant war?

XVII Chapters 29 - 33 - Luther also Stays on Course in the Work of the Reformation as Head of a Christian Family

A summarizing overview of these five chapters:
1. Marriage also for the clergy; 2. Confronting a major false intellectual leader;
3. Mission outreach; 4. Home living; 5. Congregational Worship.

XVII Chapter 29 - Luther's Marriage
Names and Places in Chapter 29

Katharina von Bora (later, Kate)   - A nun who became Martin Luther's wife

Summary of Chapter 29

A. Luther arranged for nine nuns to regain their freedom out of the Nimtzsch Convent.
B. Luther's match-making attempt seemed to have backfired.
C. Luther seemed to have become persuaded by Katharina's honest and frank response.
D. Luther's prayerful procedure, in 3 months of time, from bachelorhood to marriage proposal
   1. To honor the state of marriage;
   2. To prevent slander from spreading.
E. Notes about the two different wedding rings:
F. Luther and Kate set the example for Christian family life, also for the clergy.

Questions about Chapter 29

1. What was the basic sad reality about girls being committed to convents as far as age, commitment, and length of having to stay were concerned?

2. Name some of the risks involved in the effort of liberating former nuns:

3. How did Luther's match-making effort in regard to Katherine von Bora backfire?

4. What may have contributed toward Martin taking a shine toward Katherine?

5. Why did Martin and Kate rush into marriage after only three months of courting?

6. How many days after the marriage service of Martin and Kate was the reception dinner?

7. Where and when had the law been made that monks and nuns are not allowed to get married physically. (Perhaps you may be able to google for the answer under "11th century massive divorce" under Roman Catholicism)

8. What is the story about the wedding rings for Martin and Kate?

XVII Chapter 30 - Confronting the Intelligence-based Theologian Erasmus

Names and Places in Chapter 30

Erasmus — A celebrated intellectual of the western world

Summary of Chapter 30

A. It started with Luther's publication: "About the Babylonian Captivity".

B. Erasmus was acclaimed as the highest ranking intellectual in philosophy and theology at that time.

C. Erasmus was undecided at first, whether to support Luther or oppose him.

D. Erasmus got goaded into writing his Diatribe against Luther's Bible-based teaching of man's total spiritual corruption.

E. Over a year later, Luther ripped Erasmus' logic to pieces with his response of "The Bondage of the Will" or, "Free Will (toward conversion or salvation) Does not Exist."

F. Luther rejoiced about the fact that God did not leave the choice up to him for contributing toward his salvation.

G. It is pure fallacy that Luther changed his position later during his life time.

Questions about Chapter 30

1. (B) Who was Erasmus?

2. (B) Why was Martin Luther a problem for Erasmus?

3. (C) What might you say was Erasmus' major problem?

4. Why had Pope Leo X given the title "Defender of the Faith" to King Henry VIII?

5. (D) Why did King Henry VIII goad Erasmus into writing against Luther?

6. What might be thought to have been Erasmus' major mistake in his "Diatribe" against Luther's teaching about conversion and salvation? Perhaps the explanations of the Second and Third Article of the Apostles' Creed may be reviewed in this context.

7. (F) Why was Luther glad that God did not leave it up to him to participate for gaining salvation?

XVII Chapter 31 - The Reformation, Spreading in Wider Circles

Names and Places in Chapter 31

Margrave Albrecht of Brandenburg — Became head duke of Prussia in 1525
Rigo, Reval, Dorpat, Danzig — cities in Prussia and Latvia, north-east of Saxony
Henry Voes and John Esch — Augustinian co-workers at Brussels, who became first martyrs for the cause of the Reformation

Summary of Chapter 31

A. The gospel spread to many cities in Germany.
B. It also spread to neighboring territories and countries.
C. Luther would not let it spread by way of compromise.
D. Luther wrote the special commemorative hymn for the two martyrs in the Netherlands.
E. There was persecution also in many other locations. (More in chapter 36)
F. Luther's "love and laments" at the death of Staupitz in 1524.

Questions about Chapter 31

1. By what outward means did God cause the gospel to spread to many cities, territories, and countries?

2. By what spiritual means did the whole reformation movement happen at Luther's time?

3. (C) What did God not allow Luther to apply in the spreading of the gospel?

4. (F) About what did Luther both "love and lament", when he heard about the death of Staupitz?

5. How was the death of Voes and Esch different from the death of Staupitz?

XVII Chapter 32 - From the Family Home of the Reformer

Names and Places in Chapter 32

Link	- Luther's co-worker and preacher at Nuernberg
Lange	- Luther's co-worker and preacher at Erfurt
Hans and Elizabeth	- First two children of Martin and Kate

Summary of Chapter 32

A. Elector John gave the former Augustinian Monastery building to Luther.

B. Luther briefly tried his hand at garden work, and also at carpentry.

C. Luther's only source of monetary income was 200 guilders from the elector, about $26,264 in 2015 [?], and Kate's faithful and ambitious excellent home management.

Note: According to Schwiebert's <u>Luther and His Times</u> a Rhenish guilder in 1536 was valued at $13.40 in 1950 U.S. dollars. ($1 in 1950 is $9.8 in 2015 according to the Dave Manuel Inflation Calculator [via www.])

D. Luther had a near death experience in 1527. This was also followed by the plague which drove the university faculty out of Wittenberg.

E. Martin's and Kate's first three children:

F. Take a look at Martin Luther's extra occupations!

Questions about Chapter 32

1. For what purpose had the home of Luther served before the Elector gave it to him?

2. Who was the better gardener, Martin or Kate?

3. (C) How high was Luther's monetary income after his marriage; before his marriage?

4. (D) What was the probable physical cause of Luther's near death in 1527?

5. (E) Name Martin and Kate's first three children:

6. (F) Name some of the extra duties, besides preaching, which occupied Martin Luther.

XVII Chapter 33 - With a New Church Service

Names and Places in Chapter 33

Johann Walter and Konrad Rupf — Men gifted in music to help Luther with their music knowledge in planning for the first Lutheran church service

Summary of Chapter 33

    A. Luther's working relationship with the new Elector was excellent.
    B. Luther was given the assignment to design a new Sunday worship service in German.
    C. Time of day and design of regular services are explained.
    D. Previous congregational worship services under Romanism had been deplorable.

Questions about Chapter 33

1. (A) How was Luther getting along with the new Elector?

2. (B) What special project did the Elector assign to Luther?

3. For how many worship services did Luther officiate per week?

4. In what way was exorcism connected with baptism in the earlier Lutheran church services?

5. Is there still a connection between baptism and exorcism? (Perhaps Acts 26:18 might be considered.)

XVIII Chapters 34 - 37 - Out of the More Peaceful Situations Into Severe Stormy Situations

XVIII Chapter 34 - Church Visitations to Determine the Spiritual Condition of Congregations and Pastors in Saxony

Summary of Chapter 34

A. Plans for advancing the gospel ministry were desperately needed.
B. The Elector and Luther devised strategy for visitations.
C. Luther published, "German Mass and Order for Divine Service Undertaken at Wittenberg." The Elector directed other pastors to use this form for church service.
D. Melanchthon was to devise a plan for continuing the visitations. This plan was published with a foreword by Luther in Feb. 1527.
E. Luther, Jonas, and 3 lay members were injected into the program as a visitation team, July, 1528.
F. Scary results were reported by visitors. Counter measures were applied.
G. Luther had to be recalled to continue his work at the university.

Questions about Chapter 34

1. Why was it necessary to make church visitations?

2. What special information did the Elector and Luther seek to obtain with these visitations?

3. What was the special writing by Luther, with which the congregations were urged to acquaint themselves and possibly adopt the same for use in their congregations?

4. (E) How many were on Luther's team, when he was also requested to serve as a visitor in 1528?

5. (F) What abominable findings did Luther report?

6. (F) Name the two counter measures, which were put into practice:

7. (G) Why did Luther have to be recalled from visiting to lecturing at the university?

XVIII Chapter 35 - Luther's Catechisms
Summary of Chapter 35

A. Luther deplored how the common people abused the new gospel freedom.

B. From 1520 to 1529 Luther had been developing basic thoughts for a minimum absolute confession of faith to which every Christian should subscribe.

C. In 1929 the Large Catechism was printed and was being firmly promoted.

D. The first edition of the Small Catechism followed the same year. A few phrases and parts were added to the Small Catechism during the following two years.

E. The basic structure of the two Catechisms has been appreciated for general use by generations of Christians for at least the following 5 centuries.

F. Luther gave a comforting assessment to Elector Hans. (Note: The nickname, Hans, is derived from the full Biblical name "Johannes", "John" is the English version.)

Questions about Chapter 35

1. How was the new gospel freedom being abused by commoners?

2. (B) For how many years had Luther been occupying himself with determining what basic Bible knowledge commoners should have, before the Catechisms were printed?

3. (C) Which Catechism came off the press first?

4. (D) What were some of the phrases and/or parts which were added to revised editions during the next two years?

5. What was Luther's Small Catechism also called in the book?

63

XVIII Chapter 36 - Persecution of the Church within the Empire

Names and Places in Chapter 36

Bailiff Aichill	- a killer who hanged 40 evangelical preachers in Swabia and Franconia
Georg of Frundsberg	- field commander of a smaller German army, which in 1527 marched against Rome, conquered the city and actually occupied the conquered city for a short time
Leonhard Kaesar	- Lutheran preacher in Bavaria who was burned at the stake in August, 1527
Elisabeth Joachim	- The wife of Elector Joachim of Brandenburg, who was imprisoned by her husband because she received the Lord's Supper the Lutheran way, and defended the Lutheran communion service. She succeeded, with help of her brother, to break out and flee to Saxony
Ratzeberger	- Became the Elector's personal doctor. He was also a trusted friend of Luther
Caesar Charles V	- The central most bitter enemy, determined to "exterminate the Lutheran sect"

Summary of Chapter 36

A. Rage was being vented against gospel confessors after the Peasant War.

B. Nine martyrs at Bamberg; the action by bailiff Aichill in Swabia; the renewed issued threat by Caesar Charles V. Also recall [chapter 31 – D] the two martyrs in the Netherlands.

C. Plans began being laid for unifying the Evangelicals.

D. Important meetings took place in 1526.

    1. In February the Evangelicals met at Gotha to form what was to become the Torgau Alliance. Luther was firmly opposed to the forming of this alliance.

    2. The first Diet of Speyer began May 1st. Caesar was determined to clean up the "damned Lutheran teaching".

E. Luther misjudged the leanings of King Henry VIII and Duke George and was embarrassed.

F. Duke George also misjudged an excellent treatise and was embarrassed.

G. Elector John made a grand entry into Speier. He displayed his coat of arms.

H. Huge concessions were made toward the Evangelicals by the delegates and also by Caesar.

I. The motion, which was very favorable for the Evangelicals, was adopted by the Diet. The heads of government were to determine which religion could be used in their territories.

J. A short-lasting actual conquest of the city of Rome by a German (mercenary {?}) army happened.

K. Philip of Hessen wanted to launch a fast reformation in his territory. Luther cautioned against haste. The landgrave accepted Luther's advice.

L. More martyrdom was applied against the confessors of the gospel in Bavaria.

M. A gospel preacher was murdered at Halle.

N. Elector Joachim of Brandenburg imprisoned his wife, Elisabeth, on account of the gospel. With some help Elisabeth escaped to Saxony.

O. Once more Duke George voiced his rage against Elector John on account of the gospel.

P. The scam artist, Otto von Pack, deceived Philip of Hessen. It was Luther's strong advice which prevented an outbreak of war.

Questions about Chapter 36

1. (A,B,N,) Name three places or territories where gospel confessors were being martyred: (Look for your answer to the Summary section of this chapter.)

2. (E) In what way had Luther misjudged King Henry VIII and Duke George?

3. (F) In what way had Duke George misjudged the pamphlet, "Whether Soldiers Can also Be Saints"?

4. (H & I) What huge concession did the first Diet of Speyer make toward the Evangelicals?

5. (J) What actually happened to the city of Rome in 1527?

6. (N) Why did Elector Joachim of Brandenburg have his wife, Elisabeth, imprisoned?

7. Why was Caesar Charles V a very dangerous enemy against the gospel truth?

8. (P) With what scam did Otto von Pack deceive Count Philip and also Elector John?

9. (P) What was the advice of Luther which prevented the outbreak of war against Catholicism?

XVIII Chapter 37 - The Evangelicals Becoming the Protéstants

Names and Places in Chapter 37

Oecolampad, Zwingly, Carlstadt, Bucer, Capito — All of these were of the more liberal Swiss reformation movement. Luther and all the Wittenberg theologians stood opposed to them, because the Swiss theologians used reason quite liberally for interpretation of more difficult Bible doctrines, of which the Sacraments were in more central focus at that time. (Example: In regard to Holy Communion they kept insisting that "signifies" must be understood in place of "is". They regarded the Sacraments as symbolic actions, not as acts by which the Holy Spirit creates and strengthens the faith in Christ in the hearts of Christian believers.

Summary of Chapter 37

A. On February 21, 1529, the second Diet of Speyer began.

B. Luther had written a treatise for all Germans to fight for Caesar against the Turks.

C. The first convention business was the adoption of a motion that the resolution of the Diet of Speyer in 1526 be retracted, and contrary measures become law.

D. King Ferdinand declared that the new resolution stood adopted. He and the imperially appointed delegates left the assembly.

E. The evangelical minority drafted a protest, and when that failed, a document of appeal.

F. A preliminary contract was drawn up among the Evangelicals right after, which was to be further discussed in June at Rotach (and that would lead to the establishing of a defense alliance among the Evangelicals).

G. Luther did not agree with such procedure. Rather amidst such stormy turmoil Luther put his trust in God into words with the writing and composing of the "Mighty Fortress" anthem.

Questions about Chapter 37

1. (B) With what message had Luther urged all Germans in 1528 with his writing, "Concerning the War against the Turks"?

2. (A & C) What was the first convention action of the second Diet of Speier in February, 1529?

3. (E) With what two main statement did the evangelical lords respond to the newly adopted resolution by the diet?

4. (F) What else did the Evangelicals do in response to the newly adopted resolution of the diet?

5. (G) What special hymn did Luther write and compose during those threatening times?

XIX Chapters 38 - 39 Battling against Right Wing Reformers
XIX Chapter 38 - The Swarming Sacramentarians

Summary of Chapter 38

A. Returning to the 2nd part of Luther's writing, "Against the Heavenly Prophets," in reference to Carlstadt Luther included:
  1. The exposure of Frau Hulda, the human intellect, applying reason over God's Word.
  2. When reason is applied over God's Word, soon no articles of faith remain.
  3. Correction of Carlstadt's false interpretation of John 6:63; Christ's words that "The flesh counts for nothing." Jesus did not say, "My flesh counts for nothing."
  4. Luther insisted that we dare not stray from Scriptures' words as they are stated.
B. Luther's writing against Carlstadt applied to the Swiss reformer, Zwingli, as well.
C. A summary of Zwingli's life and his position against Rome:
D. Zwingli's position in regard to the doctrine of the real presence of Christ in the bread: That he changed the word "is" to "signifies" showed clearly in his book, "About the True and False Religion."
E. Zwingli had a deceiving dream on April 13, 1525.
F. Zwingli's application of reason in the Lord's Supper controversy also began to apply in reference to the value of Baptism and to original sin.
G. Oecolampad, Capito and Bucer, Schwenkfeld and Krautwald were using the same reason-over-Scripture method as Zwingli.
H. Luther provided a classic summary of Swiss reformed entanglements re. the Lord's Supper:
I. Two basic errors are pointed out in regard to the interpretation by the south German theologians:
J. Luther's "Sermon about the Sacrament …" ignited a longer exchange of polemical writings.
K. Zwingli's response, "A Friendly Forbearance and Declining (Fruendliche Verglimpfung und Ableining)
L. Luther's longer writing (Spring, 1527) "That These Words of Christ: 'This Is My Body' still Stand Firm against the Swarmers' Spirit," noting
  1. That the devil is behind all of this
  2. Luther's classic definition of a heretic's obstinacy
  3. What Luther's writing might accomplish:
     (a) Some students would be informed and, perhaps, corrected;
     (b) The weak could be strengthened and preserved;
     (c) Luther would have left a witness for all; and
     (d) To despise the devil.
M. Zwingli responded, "An Amicable Commentary about Dealing with the Evening Supper."
N. A second response by Zwingli: "That These Words of Christ: 'This Is My Corpse' etc. Will Have Their Own Meaning Eternally, and What Luther with His Last Book, and the Pope's Understanding Did not at All Teach or Prove."
O. Luther's final large conclusion for the whole controversy (March 1528): "Confession of the Supper of Christ."
P. Carlstadt at last found a home with the Swiss reformers.

Questions about Chapter 38

Note: Luther's phrase of "Frau Hulda" referred to human reason as an enemy of God. In his commentary on the 1st Commandment Luther called Hulda a devil. He also referred to Hulda as a witch.
(Reference for this: Luther's Saemmtliche Schriften, Vol III, pp. 1150 and 1156)

1. (A) Name two bad consequences that would result, if human reason were allowed to interpret difficult Scripture passages.

2. (B) With what other gospel preacher did Luther compare Carlstadt?

3. (See the first 14 of the Marburg Articles) In what respect were Luther's and Zwingli's teachings similar?

4. (D, E, F,) In what way was Luther opposed to Zwingli's teachings?

5. (I) On what two false premises did the Swiss reformers built their denial of the real presence of Christ's body and blood in Holy Communion?

6. (L – 3) Name several reasons why Luther wrote, "Confession about the Supper of Christ?"

7. (P) Where did Carlstadt finally find a home to stay?

XIX Chapter 39 - The Marburg Colloquy

Note: A colloquy is a discussion between formerly or current opposing sided persons or groups to establish agreement or disagreement about vital issues.

Summary of Chapter 39

A. Luther informed the Elector that alliance with the southern cities would involve alliance with false teaching.

B. The convinced Elector John instructed the Wittenberg attendees to only listen at the Rotach meeting and then report back to him.

C. The Swiss theologians' goals, with the assumption that Philip of Hessia was on their side, wanted to also win over Elector John and Markgrave of Brandenburg.

D. Philip invited the Wittenbergers to a non-debatable friendly discussion for unity. The Wittenberg theologians regarded Zwingli and Philip of Hessia politicians of the same feather.

E. Zwingli set out for Marburg at dusk. He was joined by Oecolampad, Bucer, Hedia and Sturm, arriving at Marburg Sept. 29th. Luther came with Melanchthon, Cruciger, and Mykonius. They were yet joined by Osiander, Brenz and Agricola.

F. The Colloquy took place October 2nd to 3rd in German, not Latin. Only the higher educated were invited.

   1. Zwingli and Oecolampad did most of the debating for the southerners.

   2. Luther did almost all of the debating for the Wittenbergers. He wrote the words, "This is my body," with chalk under the table cloth, determined not to be detached from these words.

   3. They restricted their discussion to the doctrine of the Lord's Supper only. The main issues under scrutiny revolved around Zwingli's false interpretation of John 6:63 and the doctrines of Christ's omnipresence and omnipotence.

G. The concluding assessment included that a friendly spirit had prevailed. One flare-up had occurred. Luther had yielded nothing to reason.

H. Philip of Hessen got everyone to sign a mutual confession in regard to 14 different doctrine points, which had not been discussed. They also defined somewhat on what parts of point 15 they had agreed. Point 15 was about the Lord's Supper.

I. Luther would not, nor could he, share a brotherly hand shake, since both sides were governed by different spirits. The whole Wittenberg team stood united with one another. Luther acknowledged that the love which he showed, was really no different than a Christian's love toward his enemies.

J. Note the different kinds of reports which both sides reported back to their home base.

K. A facsimile of 10 signatures that were given under the Marburg Articles.

Questions about Chapter 39

1. (A) Why was Luther against a political alliance which was to include cities of southern Germany?

2. (D) In what way did the Wittenberg theologians regard Philip of Hessia and Zwingli as being in full agreement with each other?

3. (F) Who were the four main debaters at the Marburg Colloquy?

4. (F – 2) From which four words did Luther never want to be separated?

5. (F – 3) Which two false teachings about the Lord's Supper did the Swiss reformers refuse to let go?

6. (G) In regard to what use of reason did Luther yield absolutely nothing in the Marburg Colloquy?

7. How many theologians signed the Marburg Articles? Can you discern their names?

8. (I) For what purpose could Luther not exchange handshakes with the Swiss reformers?

9. (J) In what way did reports at home base of the two opposing sides at Marburg differ?

XX Chapter 40 - Coburg and Augsburg
Names and Places in Chapter 40

Philip of Hessia	- The head of government in the territory of Hessia, west-south-west of Saxony
Melanchthon, Jonas, Spalatin and Agricola	- Were on the Wittenberg team with Luther, as the group was heading for the Augsburg Diet. Luther was left at the Coburg (about half way between Wittenberg and Augsburg) for security reason, while the Elector and some of his staff and the Wittenberg theologians continued to Augsburg.
Veit Dietrich and Cyriakus Kaufmann	- were left at the Coburg with Luther as his companions.
Urbanus Regius and Martin Bucer	- Two theologians who visited Luther during his 6 months' stay at the Coburg. They were deeply impressed.
Christian Beyer	- The chancellor of Saxony who served to read the prepared Lutheran Confession at Augsburg with a loud voice before the royal assembly from 3:00-5:00 PM on Saturday, June 25, 1530.

Summary of Chapter

A. To the dismay of Philip of Hessia, an alliance for armed opposition against Caesar could not be formed because of Luther.

B. Luther's powerful sermon to all of Germany to support Caesar Charles V, against the common enemy of all Christendom, namely, the Turk or Islam, shows Luther's submission to higher authority.

C. On January 21, 1530, Charles V announced that the Diet of Augsburg would begin April 8th.

D. Elector John Frederick began to prepare March 12th and 13th right after he had received the invitation,
   1. Requesting the counts, who were his spiritual brothers, to attend at the Diet;
   2. Requesting the Wittenberg theologians to set up clearly stated articles and submit them by March 18th.

E. The theologians submitted their essays together with the Marburg - Schwabach Articles about March 21st.

F. The Elector left Wittenberg April 3rd. Some theologians joined the Elector's traveling group at the Coburg on April 23rd. The Coburg was about half way between Wittenberg and Augsburg. It was still in the Elector's governmental territory. Luther had to stay at the Coburg for security reason with his table partner, Veit Dietrich, and student Cyriakus Kaufmann for company.

G. While staying at the Coburg Luther intended to build three shrines.

H. Luther's allagory, comparing the Augsburg lordships with the kingdom of the birds:

I. Luther occupied himself with translating almost all the rest of the prophets and interpreting some special Psalms.

J. Luther gave the reason why he wanted to build a shrine for Aesop.

K. Luther wrote the sharp "Admonition to the Spiritual Leaders Gathered at Augsburg for the Imperial Diet".

L. Luther also produced the writing at the Coburg, "About the Interpretation of Holy Scripture, and the Intercession of the Saints," including:
   1. His explanation for inserting the word "alone" in Romans 3:28, and
   2. His far superior translating skill, comparing himself somewhat to the Apostle Paul, when Paul in reference to the so called super-apostles explained his qualification as a truly qualified Apostle in 2. Corinthians 11-12.

M. He also produced the writing at the Coburg, "That Children Should Be Kept in School."

N. While having to endure severe physical as well as spiritual pains some more writings:
O. Other occupation included:
   1. In-depth prayer life;
   2. News of the death of his father;
   3. Reacting to many visitors, including the distinguished theologian, Urbanus Regius.
P. He wrote many letters, including the one to his son, Hans, and received mail from Kate.
Q. However, most of the thoughts, with which he occupied himself, were about Augsburg:
   1. With the rod and staff of God in his hand;
   2. With intensive supplications from the heart;
   3. With encouragements to the Wittenberg team at Augsburg.
R. Luther approved the revision of the Augsburg Confession, which the Elector sent to him, and gave an answer to the Elector's other question.
S. Caesar arrived at Augsburg on June 5th:
   1. He repeated his request to the Lutheran preachers not to preach in the meantime,
   2. But he also then felt obligated to allow some latitude.
T. The Wittenberg theologians refused to participate in the royal procession, which included bowing in submission, as the elevated host was passing by during the procession.
U. Note the two-way blockade against writing letters.
V. Luther scolded Melanchthon in regard to his philosophical depression.
W. The Imperial Diet was opened on June 20th. The hearing of the Confession of faith by the Evangelicals was to take place on June 24th, but had to be postponed to the 25th, on account of too much other business.
X. The Saxon Vice Chancellor, Christian Beyer, read the Confession with a loud voice, heard outside as well as inside, on the 25th, from 3:00 to 5:00 PM.
Y. At the first hearing of the news Luther expressed overflowing joy.
Z. Impressions at large were twofold. Luther also wrote a special letter to the Archbishop of Mainz, as to a Gamaliel. (See Acts 5:34-40 [NIV])
AA. The refutation, which was ordered to be written by opponents, turned out to be a pure sham(e).
BB. Philip of Hessia deliberately rode off in protest.
CC. A special commission of 7 men from each side, which was later reduced to 3 men from each side, was appointed. Luther wrote a sharp warning to the Wittenberg team and also wrote a softer message to the Hessians.
DD. Melanchthon seemed to begin compromising while debating and re-writing and was under fire from both directions.
EE. Caesar concluded the diet with an irrational closure, which the Evangelicals refused to accept. The Evangelicals were given the deadline of April 15, 1531, to submit to Rome.
FF. The Elector bade farewell and left.
GG. Prince John Frederick reached the Coburg first and offered Luther to travel back home with him. Luther declined, preferring to await the Wittenberg team and the Elector.
HH. Luther wrote a blunt, but also very comforting, letter to the elector, and joined the Wittenberg troop homeward on October 5th.
II. The footnote about the two displays, the ring and Luther's coat of arms.
JJ. After preaching at Altenburg Luther gently chastised the ambitious Melanchthon.

Questions about Chapter 40

1. (A) What was Luther's main objection to the forming of an armed alliance against Caesar Charles V?

2. (B) In what other way did Luther keep supporting Caesar, though Caesar wanted to destroy Luther?

3. Who is meant with the phrase, "The hand which would remain free"?

4. What is meant with the phrase, "What kind of weather he would provide"?

5. (D) How did Elector John Frederick begin to prepare for the Imperial Diet at Augsburg?

6. (F) Where were Coburg and Augsburg located in relation to Berlin and Wittenberg?; also, see the map on p. 90 of this Study Guide.

7. (F) Why did the Elector leave Luther at the Coburg?

8. (G) For what purpose did Luther want to build three shrines, while he would stay at the Coburg?

9. (H) With what kingdom did Luther compare the lordships at Augsburg? If time permits, read paragraphs two and 3 on p. 297.

10. (I) What did Luther undertake in regard to Holy Scripture, while he was at the Coburg?

11. (J) Why did Luther dedicate one of his imaginary shrines to Aesop?

12. (K) What special advice did Luther give to the spiritual lordships assembled at Augsburg?

13. (L - 1) Why did Luther insert the word "alone" into his translation of Romans 3:28?

14. (L – 2) How did Luther compare his translating skill with the Apostle Paul's qualifications for being a true Apostle?

15. (M) Why did Luther think it very important that children receive a good education?

16. (N, O, P,) With what other projects did Luther occupy himself during the 5 months and 20 days he stayed at the Coburg?

17. Take a guess! To what might "God's Rod and Staff in his hand" refer, and how might that be further understood?

18. (R) What was the other question for which the Elector was asking Luther to give an answer?

19. (T) Why did the Wittenbergers refuse to participate in the royal procession, which was also carrying the elevated host?

20. (U) What was the two-way blockade of letter writing?

21. (V) Once the blockade was lifted, of what did Luther accuse and scold Melanchthon?

22. (X) On what date was the Confession of the Evangelicals read before the assembled royalties at Augsburg; and how long did the reading last?

23. (Z) Why did Luther compare the Archbishop of Mainz with Gamaliel in his special letter to this archbishop?

24. (AA) Why was the Refutation, which Charles V ordered, such a sham?

25. (CC) What was Luther's sharp warning, while the participants of the appointed arbitration commission were haggling?

26. (CC) What only way did Luther figure that the whole discussion of the commission could end?

27. (DD) What was happening to Melanchthon during those extended negotiations?

28. (EE) Why was Caesar's closure, which the Evangelicals refused to accept, irrational?

29. (GG) Which of the Torgau-based Saxon royalties arrived first at the Coburg on their homeward Journey?

30. (HH) Let's read the summary of Luther's comforting letter to the Elector as printed on p. 311:

31. (JJ) How did Luther gently chastise Melanchthon at Altenburg on their homeward journey?

XXI Chapters 41 - 43

God Continued to Bless the Reformation Movement
As God Provided His Peace Corps in Time of National Crisis
2. Not by a Political Christian Free Council
3. Yet, By a Temporary Concord at Wittenberg

XXI Chapter 41 - The Turk, God's Peace Corps for the Reformation

Names and Places in Chapter 41

Ferdinand	- Brother of Caesar Charles V. He was also elected as King of Rome.
Suleiman Pasha	- The Sultan of the Turkish army, which was advancing with a far larger army to overpower the divided empire army and to enslave the whole Holy Roman Empire.

Summary of Chapter 41

A. Caesar's closure of the Diet of Augsburg was declared on November 19, 1530. The April 15, 1531 deadline was also kept in place. The Imperial Chamber Court was determined to enforce the terms which Caesar had attached to the given deadline.

B. The Evangelicals realized themselves forced to form an alliance. The dukes and counts proceeded to do so on December 22, 1530.

C. The Wittenberg theologians did not interfere in regard to the decision by the lawyers. A Military Alliance for defending themselves formed in March 1531 at Smalcald in case any one of them would be attacked. Several south German cities were allowed to join.

D. Luther addressed the German lay people with two special editorials, stating plainly that the Augsburg Edict was a work full of lies.
   1. In his first writing Luther pointed to Hus' Swan Prediction as a prophecy.
   2. With his second writing Luther explained how individual citizens were to react.

E. The April 15, 1531 deadline passed quietly. The politicians knew that they had to yield to the Evangelicals because of the threatening Turk invasion. The empire partners needed to be united. Charles V obviously had to agree.

F. A peace treaty within the empire was completed by June 23, 1532 at Nuernberg.

G. In appreciation a German army of 80,000 held the Sultan Pasha with his 250,000 at bay near Vienna. The Turk, seeing renewed unity in Germany, retreated.

   (Another event also is said to have happened. A German army using an unexpected strategy with the loading of their canons, which threw the massive Turk aggression into confusion, and which contributed considerably toward the Turk's retreat.)

H. Elector John died August 16, 1532. Luther preached for the funeral service.

I. A big upswing of the reformation movement, which was spreading ever wider, was being realized. The Province of Pommerania (*Pommern in German*) from which the ancestry of many early WELS (Wisconsin Evangelical Lutheran Synod) members emigrated, joined the other reformation provinces.

Questions about Chapter 41

1. For what purpose had Caesar issued a deadline?

2. (B & C) What were the Evangelicals forced to do rather quickly after the Diet of Augsburg?

3. (D) See if you can cite three main points Luther made in his editorials for German citizens:

4. (E) Why could Caesar's given deadline not be enforced?

5. (F) On what date was a peaceful solution for the Roman empire reached?

6. (G) What caused Sultan Pasha with his 250,000 troupes to retreat from Vienna?

7. (H) Can you still distinguish between the three Frederick electors, perhaps by the names and their years of serving as electors? (See the note between chapters 27 and 28 of this compendium.)

8 (I) How did the internal peaceful conditions within the empire favor the spread of the reformation?

9. Read the last paragraph of this chapter and see if you can recognize a connection with at least some ancestors of WELS.

10. The second **dedicated** Elector Frederick was called to his home in heaven on August 15, 1532. Luther had the privilege of preaching for that funeral service

XXI Chapter 42 - A Free Christian Council (?)
Names and Places in Chapter 42

Cardinal Vergerius — A papal delegate, who was sent to Wittenberg to negotiate with the Elector and with Luther about the next place for holding a church council

Paul III — was crowned as pope in 1532 after Clemens VII had died

Bullinger — One of Zwingli's followers

Summary of Chapter 42

A. Pope Paul III succeeded in the papal office after the death of Pope Clemens VII.

B. Legate Cardinal Vergerius visited Wittenberg to explore Luther's possible desire for a church council. Luther deliberately dressed sharply for that meeting for a purpose.

C. The Smalcald League was growing. However, King Franz of France and King Henry VIII of England were not admitted as members for reason.

Questions about Chapter 42

1. (B) What did legate Cardinal Vergerius want to accomplish with his visit to Wittenberg?

2. What special change happened in the life of Cardinal Vergerius by 1542?

3. (C) Why was the admission of King Franz of France and King Henry VIII of England to the Smalcald League not granted?

XXI Chapter 43 - The Temporary Wittenberg Concord

Summary of Chapter 43

A. Bucer of Strassburg, heading a delegation of several south German cities, desired to join the Lutheran reformation movement already as early as in 1530, when Luther was at the Coburg.

B. Zwingli and Oecolampad, two Swiss reformation leaders, met death rather suddenly.

C. Bucer and Melanchthon seemed to have reached theological agreement in Dec. 1534.

D. Luther was open to a meeting for discussion in May, 1536. The meeting was postponed to the 21st of May to be held at Eisenach, due to Luther's physical weakness at the time. When that also did not work out, the delegation from South Germany travelled straight to Wittenberg.

E. After sufficient discussion, involving two larger groups, a concord was declared.

F. Note Luther's comment about the difference between Luther's and Bucer's kind of preaching.

G. Later Luther had to face the facts that the Swiss just did not want to let go of the Zwinglian doctrine.

Questions about Chapter 43

1. (A) Which 4 south German cities wanted to be members of the Lutheran reformation?

2. (B) What caused the death of Zwingly?

3. (D & E) On what date did Bucer and associates reach agreement with the Lutheran theologians?

4. On what point of doctrine had Luther wanted to be very clear in the discussions with the southern German theologians?

5. (F) What did Luther point out in friendly conversation was the difference between Bucer's and Luther's preaching?

XXII Chapters 44- 45 - Building on Solid Confessional Foundation for Further God-Guided Reformation Expansion

XXII Chapter 44 - The Smalcald Articles, Hailed as Luther's Solid Testament That still Stands

Summary of Chapter 44

A. Pope Paul III announced that a council would be held at Mantua in May, 1537.
 1. One given reason: "The extirpation of the poisonous Lutheran heresy."
 2. Since Luther and Melanchthon thought it important to show their presence,
 3. The Elector directed Luther to put his doctrine into articles to be submitted to the other theologians for approval or corrections.
 4. Such a confession, if needed, was to be ready to be submitted to the next Church Council.

B. Luther had his articles in written form ready, and submitted the same to the elector by Jan. 3rd.
 1. Part I, about the majesty of God;
 2. Part II, about the office and work of Christ;
 3. Parts II and III, articles which would never be adopted by the Catholic Church, for everything in these parts was in opposition to the pope, the devil, and the world.

C. The Elector expressed his unreserved gratitude to Luther.

D. About 40 theologians met in Smalcald in February, 1537.

E. One of the bigger concerns at that meeting was the sharply deteriorating physical health of Luther.
 1. Luther had excruciating pain because of large kidney stones.
 2. Luther had resigned himself to physical death. Still, he was being moved to Gotha for so called better treatment. Along the way the bumpy road caused the stones to start passing amidst shattering pains.
 3. At first Luther felt that he was recovering. Soon, though, Luther resigned himself anew to physical death at Gotha. Yet God granted him relief and over time also recovery.

F. Bucer together with Wolfhart came to pay a visit to Luther at Gotha.
 1. Luther promised to see what he could do for them, and he did act toward supporting them.
 2. In the end, Luther had to admit that the Swiss did not want to let go of the Zwinglian doctrine.

G. The Evangelicals finally were compelled to decline attending the Council at Mantua, since they already were declared condemned without having received a hearing.

H. Luther's articles were signed by all those who had attended at Smalcald. To this day the same Articles stand as one of the key confessions of the reformation movement. Only Melanchthon registered some reservation with his signature.

I. An added submitted tract by Melanchthon in regard to the primacy of the pope was also signed by most of those theologians on the way back to Wittenberg.

Questions about Chapter 44

1. (A – 1) What was one of Pope Paul III's firm goals for the Council of Mantua in May 1537?

2. (A - 2, 3, 4,) Why did Elector John want Luther to draw up a special set of articles during the last months of 1536?

3. (B) About which Part of his articles did Luther know in advance that the Catholic Church would never agree?

4. (D) When and where did main theologians of the reformation movement meet to discuss and support Luther's teachings?

5. (E) What became the bigger concern for the Smalcald assembly in February of 1537?

6. (F) For what purpose did Bucer and Wolfhart make the special trip to Gotha to ask of Luther?

7. (G) Why did the Evangelicals finally feel compelled to decline attending the Council at Mantua?

8. (H) Why were the Smalcald Articles adopted and included as one of the main confessional writings of the Lutheran Church?

9. (I) What special treatise by Menlanchthon was also somewhat adopted by the reformation theologians?

10. (J) During what years did the third Frederick serve as Elector of Saxony?

XXII Chapter 45 - Reformation Harvesting Continued, Despite Storm Clouds Gathering at the Horizon

Names and Places in Chapter 45

George of Saxony,   - met in order to form an alliance against Lutheranism
Heinrich von Wolfenbuettel,
Erich von Kalenberg,
King Ferdinand,
and Caesar Charles V

Summary of Chapter 45

A. Duke George's sudden death happened April 17, 1539, a blessing for the reformation.
   1. Three opposing counts had started a counter-reformation alliance.
   2. As the Turk was again on the move, this new alliance could not proceed with enforcement of the Augsburg edict.
   3. Caesar Charles showed disfavor toward the Iimperial Vice Chancellor Held, who had wanted to head into battle against the Evangelicals.
   4. Duke George's two sons had preceded their father in death in 1537 and 1539. Their father also died in 1539.
   5. George's brother, Heinrich, (Henry) inherited George's throne, though George had wanted to bequeath it to Caesar and to Caesar's brother, Ferdinand.
   6. Duke George had consistently served as threatening opponent toward Luther from 1517 – 1539.
B. Luther preached at the Pleissenburg in Leipzig, Pentecost Eve, 1539, for the homage celebration.
   (The homage celebration was for the installing of the new head of government.)
   1. Erich von Kalenberg also died in 1540. Thus the Catholic alliance lost another of their members, for his widow welcomed the reformation movement to Braunschweig –Kalenberg (in the Berlin area).
   2. Caesar Charles V called for a meeting to be held at Speier, which was rescheduled to be held at Hagenau due to an approaching plague, to promise Christian equality in religion.
C. Melanchthon became very conscience sick unto death at Weimar, on his way to Hagenau.
   1. It involved Philip of Hessia marrying a second wife, for which marriage Bucer had been involved as counselor, and Melanchthon had become entangled with Bucer.
   2. Luther was called to help in regard to Melanchthon, while Cruciger was now to serve as delegate to Hagenau. Luther was very demanding of Melanchthon, that the latter start eating food or risk being put under the ban by Luther.
D. As reconciling efforts between Catholic and Evangelical theologians had been looking very favorable at Hagenau, suddenly everything bogged down when they began discussion about the mass, as Luther had forewarned.
E. Yet, the religious peace of Nuernberg was reconfirmed by Caesar.
F. The pope's announcing the Council of Trent in 1545 was accompanied with expectation that the Evangelicals would have to attend under Ceasar's request and terms. This posed another big threat in the form of another political storm against the Evangelicals.

Questions about Chapter 45

1. (A – 1) What other special religious alliance had been formed in Germany?

2. (A – 2, 3) Why could this other special alliance not start a war against the reformation alliance?

3. (A) What special event on April 17, 1539, served as very favorable for the reformation movement to thrive even more?

4. (B) To which government official did the Pentecost 1539 homage celebration apply?

5. (B – 1) What other area in Germany was also changed from Catholic to Evangelical control in support of the Reformation Movement?

6. (B – 2,) What purpose had Charles V wanted the meeting at Hagenau to serve?

7. (D) Why could a reconciliation between Roman Catholicism and the Reformation Movement never happen?

8. (B – 2) Though there could be no unity between the Catholics and the Lutherans, what favorable result did come out of the Hagenau Diet?

9. (E) What other renewed policy had favorably served the reformation movement?

10. (F) Yet, what new papal announcement posed the next big threat for the reformation movement?

XXIII Chapter 46 - Later Life Labors amidst Lots of Liabilities with Landmark Limitations

Names and Places in Chapter 46

Hans Loeser	- Stable master of the Pretsch Castle, to whom Luther was sent by the Elector for rehabilitation
Matthesius	- A house guest in the Luther home for some time
Agricola	- A co-worker of Luther at Wittenberg, until he began teaching a form of antinomianism (the teaching that there is no longer much of a need to preach God's Law). He then was called to serve as court preacher in Berlin.

Summary of Chapter 46

A. Some of the blessings during the following years, from 1532-1545:
  1. The awarding of three new doctor titles was celebrated in 1533.
  2. The plague of 1535 passed, and the university faculty returned from Jena to Wittenberg once more in February, 1536.
  3. A special charter was issued by the Elector Frederick the Magnanimus.
B. Translating and interpreting Holy Scripture was the most loved work for Luther.
  1. First, special attention to selected Psalms;
  2. Galatians also received some priority attention. Luther called it his Kate von Bora.
  3. The beginning of Luther's long interpretation of the Book of Genesis:
    a. Luther kept interpreting this book of the Bible during the last 10 years his life, 1536-1545.
    b. Note Luther's self-assessed place in his work.
  4. Luther preached on Matthew and John, while he was filling two longer lasting vacancies during the absence of Bugenhagen,
  5. Interpreting some more Psalms, especially Psalm 110, and
  6. Expanding the interpretation of the Lord's Prayer, including the 10 Commandments and the Creed for private devotion.
C. Luther wanted to be well prepared for finding commonly used language. In 1535 he sent for the latest German books, poems, songs, pictures, etc. as they had come off the press.
  1. He translated the O.T. Apocrypha and gave his assessment for using the same.
  2. The first complete Bible translation into German was issued in 1534.
  3. He worked jointly with his team of six members for regular translation revision meetings from 1539-1541 for the 1541 edition.
  4. Improvements were still being incorporated into the 1543 and the 1545 editions.
D. Nine of Luther's own hymns are highlighted under their given titles.
  1. Amidst a mushrooming expansion of many hymns being written by many authors;
  2. Luther also issued a warning against false teachings in hymns of well-sounding religious rhyme and melody, but under disguise and containing compromised teaching.
E. Luther was in battle dress, attacking the biggest abomination of the papacy in 1533.

1. "Concerning the Hidden Mass and the Ordination of Pastors" in 1533,
2. He topped this with his other big and powerful indictment of the papacy, "The Smalcald Articles" in 1537.
3. He wrote about the real identity of the Church; and
4. Once more, "Against the Papacy of Rome, Instituted by the Devil" in 1544.
5. Luther had still set for himself a threefold project for his later years with answering three basic questions.
6. As the papists issued a supposed scathing condemnation verdict against Luther, he just sat back, read it, enjoyed it and even wrote the epilogue for it.

F. Luther also still stayed in battle dress against the swarmers.
1. As early as 1533 he had issued the warning letter against the Frankfurt religion scam artists. He explained in plain words how lay people can recognize and avoid such swarmers who like to come in through the back door.
2. Still in 1544 he wrote, "A Short Confession D. Mart. Luther about the Holy Sacrament," urging the application of Titus 3:10;
3. In 1532 he had warned against the swarmers with the writing, "Concerning the Sneakers and the Corner Preachers".
4. Luther's position on the call remained the same. "No one may hold an office without a command or a call." He had applied this especially in regard to the Anabaptists of Muenster, where Carlstadt had been doing damage.

G. Luther was opposed to most Jews in general.
1. Most of them were no more than outright unbelievers and scoffers.
2. Luther issued three writings against them.

H. It was hard for Luther to go against his co-worker, Agricola. It hurt him.

I. Luther also had to confront the jurists, especially the honorable Dr. Schurf.

J. Melanchthon also has to be discussed in this connection.
1. Melanchthon seemed to want to give to the pope a rating of being a believer in Christ. Note his reservation in his signature under the Smalcald Articles; and also his treatise of the Primacy of the Pope. His later confessional damages, through the Leipzig Interim's massive concessions, leave the impression that he kept wanting to build a secret peace treaty, reconciling good with evil, Luther with the pope.
2. Luther would confront him, when he saw Philip stepping out of bounds, and Philip would usually repent.
3. Luther kept dealing with Melanchthon as with a fellow believer to the end of his life.
4. Most likely Luther never got to see Philip's correspondence with the Swiss reformers and their allies. Note the author's fitting assessment.

K. Still the gospel proclamation kept moving on.
1. Justus Jonas was instlalled as preacher at Halle.
   a. The Archbishop Albrecht was obligated to move out with his whole treasure of relics.
   b. Note Luther's sarcasm in the "New Newspaper from the Rhine."
2. Amsdorf was installed as bishop in Naumberg. Luther had set up the first installation liturgy for that service.
3. Bucer together with Melanchthon messed things up once more at Merseburg in 1544.

4. The reformation was also installed at Muenster.
 L. Wittenberg had begun to relapse quite sharply, reverting to godless life styles.
  1. Though Luther had kept reproving sin as it was in motion all along,
  2. A kind of luke-warmness had been settling along with outright godlessness.
  3. While Luther was making visitation, he wrote to Kate to sell everything and come and join him. He did not want to return to Wittenberg.
  4. The city council then sent the mayor and some of his colleagues to go after Luther and convince him to come back. They would assist him for restoring orderliness.
  5. Luther had been denouncing usury as a big evil.
  6. Church discipline was being urged to the point of withholding communion. Though common people could be corrected, the mighty lords would usually not accept it.
  7. Luther had wanted the office of the keys to be applied within congregations, but not by higher consistories.
 M. Luther had earlier responded to the theological faculty of Lyon's 32 polemical theses in defense of Roman doctrine against all the swarmers, the Swiss reformers and the Lutherans.
  1. Luther had not accepted being classed with Swiss reformers and kept holding that position.
  2. He had insisted and kept insisting that only God's Word can be used for establishing and defending Christian doctrine.
 N. Luther finally yielded in 1545 to let his writing be published as a set.
 O. Luther's precious advice for correct study of theology is still very much in place: Oratio, Meditatio, Tentatio.
 P. Take the time and read the good advice Luther gives to book writers.

Questions about Chapter 46

1. (B) What was Luther's preferred work, with which he loved to occupy himself?

2. (B – 2) Which book of the Bible did Luther love especially so that he called it my Kate of Bora?

3. (B) Name one of the Psalms which were among Luther's favorites:

4. Can you also state, why Luther favored the Psalm you picked out?

5. (C – 2) What year was the complete translation of all of Holy Scripture first printed?

6. (D) Can you name a couple of the hymns that were written by Luther?

7. What warning did Luther issue in reference to hymn writing?

8. (E) What did Luther name as the biggest abomination of the papacy?

9. (F) To whom was Luther referring, when he spoke about religious swarmers?

10. (G) Why did Luther write against the Jews?

11. How many opponents of Luther can you name?

12. (H) In what way was Luther hurt by Agricola?

13. (K – 1) Where was Justus Jonas installed as preacher?

14. (K – 1 - a) Why did Archbishop Albrecht feel obligated to move out of one of his favorite cities?

15. (L – 3) What had Luther instructed his wife to do, when life in Wittenberg had become quite godless?

16. (L – 4) What did the elector and Luther's colleagues in conjunction with the city council of Wittenberg do to get Luther to come back?

17. (M) Why did Luther not want to be grouped with Zwinglians?

18. (O) What was Luther's special threefold advice for correctly studying theology?

19. (K – 4) Do you know how to explain what was wrong about the teaching and practice of the Anabaptists?

20. (L – 5) How ought we to apply Luther's position on usury today?

21. (J) Might we today assess Melanchthon's double role differently than Graebner did? Consider the comments by F. Bente in the Historical Introduction of the Book of Concord .

XXIV Chapters 47 - 48 - Luther's House Was Set in Order
XXIV Chapter 47 - In the Luther Home at Wittenberg
Summary of Chapter 47

A. A summary of Luther's financial and property income during his later years.

B. Luther's 3 sons: Johannes, Martin and Paul; 3 daughters: Elisabeth, Magdalena, and Margaret; and the wider family and friendship circle who lived with the Luther family.

C. Luther's in-house preaching from 1532-1534 was preserved in the form of notes by Veit Dietrich and Deacon Roerer, and was later published under Luther's House Postil.

D. Other interpretation and conversation during meal times were later compiled into Luther's Table Talk. Not all of these are reliably genuine.

E. At times there was even singing and choir activity at Luther's dinner table.

F. Eating habits and physical health care were grossly neglected.

G. Kate also had become ill repeatedly.

H. Two daughters, Elisabeth and Magdalena, died early in life. Margaret survived.

I. Luther's mother died June 30, 1531, about a year after his father had died. Luther had written comforting letters to each of them while they were still living.

J. Luther left sufficient properties to Kate in his will.

K. Personal relationship between Martin and Kate had been loving and supportive all along.

Questions about Chapter 47

In respect to the last two chapters of this biography, consider this phrase, "Set your house in order," going back to the year 1537 at Smalcald and at Borna in Luther's life, and in light of Isaiah 38:1-6.

1. (B and H) Name the six children of Martin and Kate.

2. (A) What was the approximate annual income of Martin during his last years?

3. Name some of the other valuables among the possessions in Luther's larger estate.

4. (C) What is the "Luther House Postil"?

5. What was one of Luther's favorite food items?

6. What is the title of the book in which meal time conversation in Luther's home was being preserved?

7. How many health problems can you recall occurred in Luther's life?

8. What had been some of Kate's illnesses?

9. (I) When had Luther's parents died?

10. What kind of personal relationship did Martin and Kate enjoy with each other?

11. Should you desire to figure out a current value of Luther's estate, salary, and other material resources in 1546, then refer to p. 60 of this Compendium, chapter 32, - C, about the value of a guilder during the 16th century (about 1535).

XXIV Chapter 48 - Departure for Home in Heaven
Names and Places in Chapter 48

Wolf Sieberger — A servant in Luther's home

Martin and Kate's children — Hans, Elizabeth, Martin, Paul, Magdalena and Margaret. Elizabeth and Magdalena died during their childhood years.

Summary of Chapter 48

A. Luther's last birthday celebration.
B. During the winter season (October, 1545 – February, 1546) Luther traveled to Mansfeld several times to counsel toward the reconciliation of the counts of Mansfeld, who had been at odds with each other for some time.
C. Before Luther's last leaving, professor Meier found Luther's posted note on the door to his study chamber that "The professors should be examined about the Lord's Supper."
D. Luther reaffirmed this (point C) in his last sermon at Wittenberg, issuing a warning against the light of reason vs. faith.
E. For his last stay at Mansfeld Luther wrote five letters in the span of 14 days to Kate.
F. The reconciling objective was completed on February 17th.
G. Pains kept increasing during the night. 10 persons of the nobility class joined the rest during this time.
H. A description of Luther's actual departure.
I. A description of the processional return to Wittenberg.
J. The procession to the church at Wittenberg.
K. After two funeral services at Halle, the third funeral service in Wittenberg on February 22nd.

Questions about Chapter 48

1. (A) What special advice did Luther give to his friend, Paul Eber, during Luther's last birthday celebration?

2. (B) For what purpose did Luther and some of his friends and family members travel to Mansfeld several times during the winter of 1545-1546?

3. (C and D) Why had Luther posted that special note on the door of his study chamber about an examination of the Wittenberg professors?

4. (F) On what date was the reconciliation between the counts of Mansfeld completed?

5. (E) How often did Martin write letters to his Kate during his last days at Mansfeld?

6. (G) How many persons had gathered in the middle of the night around the deathbed of Martin Luther?

7. By what process was the actual appearance of the face of Luther preserved after his death?

8. On what date and at what hour did Luther die?

9. (K) How many funeral services were conducted around the body of Luther?

One more thought

Reformation kept happening and keeps happening as our good and gracious Father in heaven preserves this world which he created. Just as important, he blesses all of us, his children, with renewal of faith in Christ Jesus, our Savior, through use of his gospel in Word and Sacraments. May he who kept guiding, protecting and strengthening his servant, Martin Luther, daily with his powerful Word also keep blessing us with his life-changing and world-changing eternal Word. Keep trusting in Jesus with your whole heart as you trust in the Father and the Holy Spirit. May this biography about one of God's guided reformers keep living in our hearts as we are living in the time frame of the historic 500th anniversary of the 16th century reformation by our God on behalf of his whole Church, as well as on behalf the world in which we live on this earth. Let all of us continue to keep thanking, praising, and giving glory to our God for his continuous gracious guidance of his Church.

TO OUR GRACIOUS TRIUNE GOD ALONE BE ALL THE GLORY!

The shaded sections describe the approximate area of the

HOLY ROMAN EMPIRE

During the 16th century

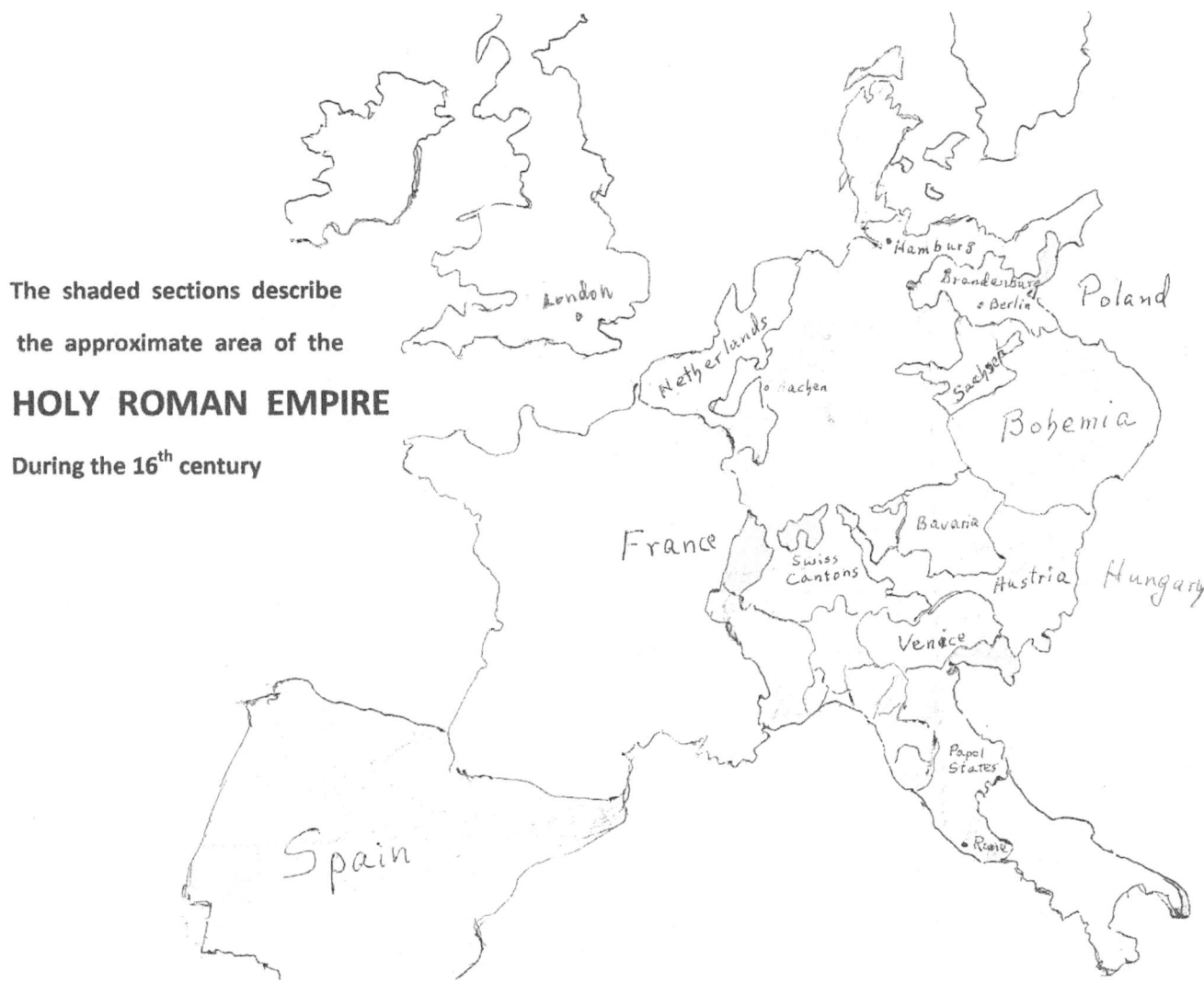

Germany 16th Century
(Approximate Boundaries and Location of Cities)

photo credit CC BY-SA 2.5, httbs://commons.wikimedia.org/w/index.php?curid871084

Approximate Locations of Luther Sites in Current Germany

Answer Guide
For 445 questions in the Study Guide for the book
-
Dr. Martin Luther 1483-1546

By Waldemar O. Loescher

I. Answers to Questions for further discussion in regard to The General Introduction for the Book, <u>Dr. Martin Luther 1483-1546</u>.

1. **What is the Public Domain?**
    A storage of formerly copyrighted items, including formerly copyrighted books. Copyright, ©, lasts for the life of the author plus 70 years. (You might Google "Public Domain" for more information)
2. **Find out how the concept of registering copyright applies to books which are not in the Public Domain.**
    Reproduction in print, or larger segments of the book, is not allowed without permission from the author or an assignee, except for allowances already stated under the copyright symbol after the title page of the book.
3. **React to the last five lines of the first paragraph under FOREWORD on p. I in the first section of the book.**

    The reading, or studying, of this book is hoped to produce a similar conviction in the mind of the reader.
4. **What is "Luther Volksbibliotek (L.V.)," translated into English, "People's Luther Library"? (See the last paragraph on p. X)**
    A shorter series of at least 25 volumes of Luther's Life and Writings (in German), which is no longer offered in print. They might be available in some personal libraries.
5. **What might you say is a major difference between Dr. Martin Luther and Dr. Martin Luther King?**
    Dr. Martin Luther was really a God-sent (God-trained, -gifted, -protected, -guided –etc.) near Christian genius to serve as spear-point leader for a much needed church reformation about 500 years ago. Dr. Martin Luther King was a Baptist political church reformer of the 20th century.
6. **How might Martin Luther's education years compare with current basic education years in our WELS current pastor-track education system?**
    See "C" in the "General Introduction for the Dr. Martin Luther Biography" (p. 2 in the <u>Study Guide</u>) and then compare with our current WELS system: Much language training besides other needed subjects etc. for 4 years of high school, 4 years of college, and 4 years of seminary. The seminary education includes one year of vicar education.
7. **Was there another writing of the 95 Theses? Yes! What was it called?**
    The 95 Resolutions, or simply "Resolutions".
8. **What is a sad reality of the approximate first half of Martin Luther's life?**
    Martin had not been taught the Gospel. He was very miserable, driven toward despair, under the teaching of God's Law. His conversion and assurance of salvation had not really begun until sometime after Martin Luther's university training.
9. **What is a usual secular assessment of Martin Luther's place in N.T. history?**
    A new phase of history began after the invention of the printing press (about the year 1450). Roman church political power was being reduced considerably. Martin Luther was a courageous and talented person who served as a leader for this purpose.
10. **What might we say is of first importance of Martin Luther's role in all of N.T. history?**
    - The Bible. Martin Luther served as leading translator of God's Word from Hebrew and Greek into the language of common people. God was providing his Word again for all, especially for His Church, in their common language.
11. **What may we regard as main needs in the 16th century Reformation of our God?**
    1. The translation of Holy Scripture into commonly used language. 2. Further exposure of the entrenched Scripture prophesied "Antichrist."

Questions and Answers for Chapter 1

1. (# C) The late Professor August L. Graebner points out that Martin's grandmother was a Lindemann. His mother was a "Zigur", or as the name is also found in some records, a "Ziegler."

   This lineage reference was provided by August L. Graebner for correctly understanding Luther's ancestry.

2. How old was Martin, when he was baptized?

   - One day.

3. (# D) What does this tell us about Martin's parents?

   They were dedicated to church life. They loved their newborn son.

4. For what was Martin being punished once during his earlier childhood?

   He had taken a nut out of a family supplies jar without asking.

5. What was Luther's advice during later years in regard to disciplining children?

   "The apple needs to be paired with the rod." Or, "Kindness needs to be paired with strictness."

6. (# G) What evidence did writer A. Graebner supply to describe the then-existing spiritual darkness?

   He referred to the church as 'a wilderness of false teaching' in reference to testifying God's Word. He pointed out that many patron saints were being promoted as mediators between God and man.

Questions and Answers for Chapter 2

1. How did Martin Luther describe his teachers and elementary school at Mansfeld later in his life?

   The teachers were like tyrants and hangmen. The schools were like prison and hell.

2. (# B in the <u>Study Guide</u>) Explain why Count Anhalt's way of repentance is called "grizzled holiness".

   The count had become a monk and was displaying himself, walking bare-footed and hooded in beggar's form, carrying the burden of a donkey himself, while the donkey walked alongside, unburdened. That was a kind of "grizzled holiness." Count Anhalt is said to have died rather young.

3. (# D) Why may we thank God that there also was some understanding of the Gospel, as we note the closure of Count Guenther's life?

   When this count died, he confessed that he wanted to leave this world only by way of his Savior's merit. So did he commit his soul into the hands of Jesus. (See John 10:28)

4. (# F) Note the noble character of Teacher Trebonius. How did his high respect for his students become fulfilled in regard to Martin Luther later in life?

   Teacher Trebonius showed honor for his students by taking off his cap as he would enter the classroom, stating that some of his students might well become important leaders later in their lives.

Questions and Answers for Chapter 3

1. (# A) Why did educators at that time divide the subjects they would teach the way they did?

   They would begin with a general philosophy course wanting their students to be on the same basic level in the pursuit of knowledge before they would teach more specific study topics.

2. (# B) Why was the need of learning Greek so important for the work Luther would do later in his life?

   Greek is currently regarded as the original language of the N.T.

3. (# D) What was one of the biggest surprises for Luther while studying at Erfurt?

   See "D" under "Summary of Chapter 3.

4. (# D) How did the ability of playing the lute enhance Luther's life during his student days?

This was one minor contributing factor which caused Martin to be recognized as a developing leader among students.

5. (# F) Why did Martin's becoming a monk affect Martin's father so negatively?

His father thought that he and his wife's future would most likely suffer. He must have hoped that his gifted son would be in a higher than average wage bracket in the future and be able to take care of his parents in their old age.

Questions and Answers for Chapter 4

1. (# A) What opinions did people at large hold in regard to monasteries?

   Generally, monasteries had a good reputation as they were thought to provide a kind of holiness. Many sinful worldly people thought to gain some spiritual benefits through them.

2. Why would such thoughts seem natural?

   Law-based sinners generally look for ways in which they can present themselves more acceptable to God.

3. (# C) Why couldn't the monastery requirements supply Martin with any comfort?

   Those requirements were intended to be structured in line with God's Law. God's Law will always confront sinners with their sins and the punishment which is due in answer to sins.

4. (# D) Let's read a couple paragraphs in class, beginning with the paragraph at the bottom of p. 27.

5. Note the father and son conversation after Luther was consecrated as priest. What strikes you as different from the way conversations in general among family members take place today?

   Answers to this question may vary.

6. (# E) Find the words with which the monks would trade their good works for food or earthly merchandise.

7. Let's do some reading about Staupitz, counseling Luther with some Gospel gems *(as presented on pp. 26-28 in the book)* **about:**
   Repentance
   Election
   Hope
   Forgivenee of sins

8. Why did a book written by John Hus confuse Luther?

   Luther had been trained to hate the memory of Hus, who was claimed to have been a heretic.

Questions and Answers for Chapter 5

1. (# A) Why did enrollment at the U of Wittenberg drop so drastically during the first 4 years?

   1. There was a shortage of funds for getting good professors. 2. A near-poverty standard of living in Wittenberg did not help.

2. (# A) How did Elector Frederick the Wise succeed in boosting financial support for his university?

   He secured permission for converting the financial support to be handled by a foundation, which was a federation of churches.

3. (# B) What was the starting salary of Martin Luther as a faculty member at the Wittenberg U?
   $0.00
4. (# C) Can you name the four steps that had to be taken to obtain a doctor title?
   Baccalaurius, Sententiarus, Licentiatus, Doctorate.

Questions and Answers for Chapter 6

1. (# A) By what means did the two monks, Luther and his monk brother, travel to Rome?
   They walked.
2. (# A) What had become a problem for the Augustinian monks?
   It seemed that some were for more strict rules, others for more lax rules. This difference had led to sharper dispute among the Augustinian monks. Luther and a co-monk were sent to Rome to obtain the counsel of the pope toward solving this problem.
3. (# B) What got the two monks into serious trouble at one of the Italian monasteries?
   The two Augustinians had been reproving the Italian monks for their licentious life style. The Italian monks had intended to kill them.
4. (# C) What is "debauchery" (another word for licentiousness) in Galatians 5:19?
   Indecency, claiming the right to live more liberally, even a more lustful pleasurable life.
5. (# D) What was "Pilate's Staircase" claimed to be and what good was it supposed to provide?
   It was claimed to be a 28 steps stairway that had been miraculously transferred from Pilate's judgment hall in Jerusalem to Rome. It was further claimed to provide 9 years of indulgence from purgatory for each step which pilgrims would climb on their knees toward the top of it.
6. (# E) What Bible passage is the Holy Spirit said to have preserved in Martin's heart and mind, on their journey to and from Rome?
   "The righteous will live by faith." (For further reference see: Rom. 1:17; Hab. 2:3-4; Gal. 3:11; Heb. 10:37-39; et al.)

Questions and Answers for Chapter 7

1. (A) Why did Staupitz's command, "obey!" have such powerful influence on Martin so that he proceeded to study for his doctor title?
   "Obedience" together with "Chastity" and "Poverty" was a part of the threefold vow which monks took at their induction into the Monastery Order. (See the top of p. 21 in the book for Luther's induction into the Erfurt Augustinian Monastery.)
2. (# A) Why had Martin tried to decline the directive to study for doctor title?
   He just wanted to remain humble.
3. (# B) Of what did the examination for obtaining a doctor title consist?
   Not long after having become a licentiate, a doctoral disputation had to be presented and accepted.
4. (# B) Classroom reading of the 4th paragraph on pp. 37-38 by the leader of the Bible class or by a member.

Questions and Answers for Chapter 8

1. (# A) What were Dr. Pollich's two predictions about Martin Luther, as he began his classroom teaching in Wittenberg?

   1. Monk Martin Luther would ultimately outshine all the other doctors. 2. Luther would overturn the doctrines which were holding sway in the universities. - Luther's teachings of Scripture were different than the universities' teachings of scholasticism in preparation for church priesthood.

2. (# C & D) Which were the first three books of the Bible on which Luther based his classroom lectures?
   - Psalms, Romans, Galatians.

3. (# E) Classroom reading again – Luther's letter to his friend Georg Spenlein :
   Paragraph 5 on p. 41 to p. 43.

4. (# I) What were some of the duties of Luther as District Visitor?
   For the answer see p. 53 in the book.

5. (# J) When Carlstadt returned from Rome, how did he find Luther's lectures different from the way they had been before?

   Luther was opposing quite a few of the teachings of the church fathers that had been passed on to him through the method of scholastic teaching as espoused by Thomas Aquinas.

6. (# K) Read the example of the 7 Theses out of Franz Guenther's disputations for baccalaurius ranking that may give you an idea as to how the sentences in a disputation (a debate) were set up. *(p. 48 in the book?.*

Questions and Answers for Chapter 9

1. (# A) If a person should want to divide the development of the teaching of purgatory into five history segments, which of the following might you rank differently?

   1. Strong penalties within church life as early as the 2nd century, with intention of following through with "true contrition". 2. Reduction of penalties upon "true contrition" as determined by the bishop. 3. Ever growing listings of penalties for a growing list of different sins. 4. Authority for assigning monetary indulgence was reserved for only the pope. 5. Applied as pay for participating in the Crusades (10th – 13th centuries), followed by special Years of Jubilee, followed by the peddling of indulgences in countries at large.

2. (# B) How and why did Archbishop Albrecht, in charge of the Roman Catholic expanded district of Mainz, seek to expedite indulgence sales in his territory?

   Under papal permission he commissioned agents who were to go out to churches in cities and town and sell them to people of all walks of life. A part of the proceeds from indulgence sales would be brought to the Archbishop which he would use for repayments on his huge debt. About half of the proceeds were to go to Rome for the continued building of the St. Peter Cathedral, and for the ongoing battle against the "Turk" (actually, the Mohammedan Religion, ever threatening to invade and dominate in Europe).

3. (# B & C) How was John Tetzel proceeding with his assignment? -

   Vigorously, wanting to raise as much money as possible; - Ingeniously, using all kinds of tricks and threats; - Viciously, supplanting the Gospel of the cross of Christ with his own invented spectacular cross.

4. (# C) Why did Martin Luther become so upset with Tetzel's selling of indulgences?
   - Because Tetzel's propaganda was grossly and destructively against Bible teachings.

5. (# C) What was the treasure of relics in the castle church of Wittenberg?

- *The many relics which Frederick the Wise had been collecting all along.* (See p. 55, and p. 201 for more information.)

6. (# D) **Who was Bishop Scultetus?**
   The Bishop of Brandenburg. (Brandenburg was located in the general area around Berlin).

7. (# D) **What was part of Dr. Luther's rebuking message to Bishop Albrecht of Mainz?**
   Remove this indulgence sale offense which endangers so many souls.

8. (# E) **With what main Bible doctrine did Dr. Martin Luther begin his 95 Theses?**
   Repentance as Jesus teaches us.

9. (# E) **What false teachings was Luther still defending in his 95 Theses?**
   Note how Luther himself later explained this when he burned a copy of the papal bull. But in 1517 he was still defending the pope as church leader, purgatory, and indulgence sales in general.

10. (# E) **Name at least five issues in the listing of selected Theses out of the 95 (pp. 57-63), with which Luther properly defended different Bible teachings.**
    Try numbers 3, 5, 7, 9. 11, or others.

11. (# E) **Besides the exposure of false repentance, what was a main evil exposed with the 95 Theses according to your opinion?**
    Possibly, the selling of forgiveness of sins for money.

12. (# F) **Why is the legendary dream of Elector Frederick the Wise so fitting for this event in history?**
    It seems to describe the whole central war within God's Church, of the blaring corruption in the church in direct violation against God's Truth, and how God protects His own children in the midst of deadly controversy.

Questions and Answers for Chapter 10

1. (# C) **What was the Kostnitz Affair; and how is the Moravian Church still connected?**
   Re the Kostnitz (or, Constance, Italy) Affair see the summary on pp. 30-31 of the <u>Study Guide</u> under "Some background information." The Moravian Church had its beginning as part of the "Bohemian Brethren" movement 100 years before Luther. Those confessors came under severe persecution and were almost wiped out. Some of them re-grouped later under Count Zinzendorf. Some also migrated to the U.S. later yet, and are still known as the Moravians.

2. (# E & F) **From what two men did Tetzel seek help for responding to Luther"**
   - From Archbishop Albrecht of Mainz and from Wimpina of Frankfurt.

3. (# G) **Why did the writing from Sylvester Mazolini of Prierio at first startle Luther?**
   He had expected support from Rome. He thought that this must be some sort of a hoax.

4. (# H) **How did Dr. Martin Luther follow through during the following months in regard to the 95 Theses?**
   He kept re-writing and correcting some of them, regarding them not in the form of a disputation but in the form of resolutions. In regard to this he especially published his "Sermon about Indulgences and Grace."

5. (# J) **Why did Psalm 110 and Luther's interpretation of the same give such comfort at this time?**
   It presents a summary of the history of God's Church on earth and presents Christ as our eternal High Priest in the order of Melchizedek.

6. (# I) **From what source did Luther derive increasing support for telling the whole truth to the world?**
   - From God's Word.

Questions and Answers for Chapter 11

1. (# A) What was the general agenda for the Augustinian Convention at Heidelberg?

    - *Church business, perhaps much like business in a convention in our times.*

2. (# B) What item did they tag onto their agenda, since Martin Luther would be attending?

    - *A disputation (debate) to be presented by Luther.*

3. (# B) What became clear to all attendees about Dr. Luther's theology from the 2 theses which are quoted in the chapter?

    Luther's theology was based on the teachings of the Holy Scripture. He distinguished clearly between the teaching of God's Law and the teaching of the Gospel of Christ. (You may refer to C.F.W. Walther's lectures on the proper distinction between Law and Gospel, in reference to 2. Timothy 2:15.)

4. (# C) In what way was the Dominican monk, Martin Bucer, impressed while listening and later also talking with Luther?

    Luther was a sharp and self-controlled presenter who spoke with conviction. He knew Scriptures very well. Luther was exciting and gave fitting answers with Scripture proof when he was challenged by anyone. No one could unseat him in his debating.

5. (# D) Why did Elector Frederick the Wise want Luther back in Wittenberg as soon as possible?

    Luther was needed as a top notch professor, who was attracting many students to his lectures.

Questions and Answers for Chapter 12

1. (# A) What was Dr. Carlstadt's objective in challenging Dr. Eck to a debate?

    Carlstadt wanted to make a name for himself.

2. (# B) Why did Dr. Luther send a copy of his Resolutions to the Bishop of Brandenburg?

    Bishop Scultetus was one of his superior in accordance with church polity (or orderliness).

3. (# B) Let's read Dr. Martin Luther's remarkable letter to Pope Leo X, which he sent along with a copy of his Resolutions.

    Read from pp. 73-75.

4. (# B) Though Luther was willing to submit to the pope in regard to almost everything, what was he not willing to take back?

    - *His statements that represented Scripture teachings.*

5. (# C) What was it that upset Luther so much about John Tetzel's criticism?

    - *The flimsy and distorting way in which Tetzel treated Holy Scripture.*

6. (# D) How did Luther completely destroy the criticism of Jacob von Hoogstraten?

    - *With a scathing rebuking letter in answer to Hoogstraten's wanting to suppress the truth with bloody violence. Hoogstraten had boldly stated that he wanted the pope to step in and execute Luther with fire or sword.*

Questions and Answers for Chapter 13

1. (# A) How did Pope Leo X show his real intentions with his actions in Rome?

    He sent a strong message to Elector Frederick the Wise that the Elector must submit to the pope's desires. Heresy was the charge against Luther. The pope appointed judges for the case. Luther was summoned to appear in Rome within 60 days.

2. (# B) Note why Luther had not answered Eck's Obelisks right away?

He had thought that Eck, or some other wise acre was not writing for the pope. Also: The Augustinian Convention at Heidelberg was, at that time, to begin very soon.

3. (# B) With what document did Luther now respond to Eck's Obelisks?

- Luther's Astorisks

4. (# B) Cite at least two points which Luther scored in his answer.

1. Luther applied Scripture for debating; Eck used the method of scholasticism. 2. Luther: "Faith justifies" and the Gospel is the power of God for salvation for all who believe. Eck's indulgence declaration does not justify, but produces only laziness.

5. (# C) Cite a couple points Luther scored in his "Sermon regarding the Ban".

A so-called ban which has been declared against a person who espouses a just cause, is actually not a ban at all, but is an honor. A person may bear such joyfully. (See Matthew 5:11-12)

6. (# E) How many of the Wittenberg faculty and student body did not stand in support of Luther?

- Only one licentiate in the study of law.

7. (# E) For what action did Luther seriously punish the Wittenberg students from the pulpit?

- For having forcefully acquired and having publicly solemnly burned 800 copies of Tetzel's theses.

8. (# F) How might Melanchthon's joining the Wittenberg faculty be viewed, similar to Aaron's and Hur's actions as recorded in Exodus 17:12?

Aaron and Hur kept holding Moses' arms up that the army of Israel would keep on winning the battle against the Amalekites. Melanchthon was a special gift for Luther. Though young, he was well educated, especially in Greek. He stood with Luther not only as an aid in language instruction but also in studying Scripture.

Questions and Answers for Chapter 14

1. (# A) Why was it in Luther's favor to receive a hearing in Augsburg rather than in Rome?

Caesar Maximilian was in charge over the German nation. Frederick the Wise had made it clear to this head of the Holy Roman Empire that Luther must get an unbiased hearing on German soil.

2. (# B) Why did previous reform-minded men not reach their goal?

1. Evidently the time in history had not yet been reached according to God's will. 2. Previously reform-minded leaders had usually been brutally eliminated by Roman church power.

3. (# B) Why did Luther keep travelling to Augsburg, though many people advised against it?

He trusted in God's protection and was also young yet, 35 years old. God provided him with the determination to stand up for the truth. As a Dr. of Holy Scripture he was well prepared against scholastic theologians.

4.(# C) Why did Luther not report to the Cardinal right after his arrival in Augsburg?

He had been strongly advised to first await a letter for protection from Caesar. He needed such so that Roman officials would not simply arrest him as a heretic and send him directly to Rome.

5. (# D) What does the Latin word R e v o c o mean?

- Take back. - In Luther's case, renounce what he was claimed by Roman church powers to have written against the teachings of the church.

6. (# D, E, F, & G) How many times did Luther and Cajetan actually meet face to face?

- On three different days

7. (# G) What did the Cardinal Cajetan's absolute unwillingness to change his pre-determined verdict tell us about his attitude toward Scripture?

He apparently had little knowledge of and little respect for Holy Scripture.

8. (# H) Let's read in class Luther's letter to Spalatin, who was a sort of mediator between Elector Frederick the Wise and Luther: *(pp. 101-104)*

9. (# I) How did Link and Staupitz, Luther's friends, show that they did not trust Cajetan?
They went home traveling separately on different roads.

10. (# J) How did Luther on Oct. 17th, with his message to the Cardinal, show that he could yield and submit to a certain extend?
Luther would have submitted, provided the opposition would discipline the loud-mouthed indulgence peddlers.

11. (# K & L) How many days did Luther still stay in Augsburg after he had sent a second message to the Cardinal?
- Two days.

12. (# L) What appeared to be implied by the Cardinal's "maintaining utter silence" in dealing with Luther?
The verdict against Luther had already been decided.

13. (# M) What request had Luther registered with his letter to Rome on Oct. 16th?
He requested a retraction of the citation of having to appear in Rome, to a court from which he could expect no just decision.

14. (# N) What did Cajetan request by letter of Oct.13th from Elector Frederick the Wise, as to what the Elector was to do with Luther?
- That the Elector would either hand Luther over to him, or send him into exile.

15. (# O) What two things astonished the Elector about the Cardinal's request in respect to himself and in respect to Luther?
1. Luther was to be handed over without having been granted an unbiased hearing on German soil. 2. What an outlandish request toward himself as one of the six (at that time) electoral counts.

16. (# P) What effect did the Elector's letter to Cajetan have on Luther, when he got to read it?
Luther was overjoyed now that he knew how his Elector stood toward him.

17. (# Q) What shams of Roman Catholicism had Luther exposed with his report (in Latin) late in 1518, wherewith he expressed direct opposition to Rome holding universal supremacy?
- That the pope has superior spiritual supremacy on earth, including over earthly governments.

18. (# R) Luther was now requesting a "Free Christian Council." What did he want such a Council to decide?
A Church Council would have to render a verdict whether or not Luther was guilty of heresy.

19. (# S) What other special writing did Luther produce and continue during those critical days?
A German Explanation of the Lord's Prayer, Intended for the Common Man.

20. (# T) How were Luther's many writings being received everywhere during that time?
A huge audience was waiting for anything that Luther would write.

21. (# U) How was Rome's declaration on Nov. 9, 1518, being received in Germany, that the treasure of indulgences was now declared as Rome's official doctrine?
It was not respected at all in Germany.

22. (# V) Of what did Luther now become ever more convinced?
The main teachings of Rome were completely out of alignment with the teachings of Holy Scripture. Luther kept putting his trust in God's counsel.

Questions and Answers for Chapter 15

1. **(# A) What had been the plan of Rome through Cajetan at Augsburg?**
   - To deport Luther to Rome as quickly as possible.

2. **(# B) How was that plan debunked?**
   Urbanus von Serralonga, a close friend of Cajetan, was a Roman nuncio, that is, a papal ambassador to a foreign country. It had been his assignment to lure Luther to report to Cardinal Cajetan as soon as possible after arriving in Augsburg, so that Luther could be arrested as a heretic and be sent to Rome. Luther's friends had advised him strongly to first await documentation from Caesar Maximilian. Then he would stand under Caesar's protective service. Luther accepted the advice of his friends, and Rome's plan was debunked.

3. **(# I) Explain how Rome showed a completely reversed approach through Miltitz.**
   Miltitz treated Luther honorably, totally different from the way Cajetan had conducted himself.

4. **What was "The Consecrated Rose?"**
   See pp. 97 and 99 in the book for the answer to this question.

5. **(# E) What did the Pope expect from Elector Frederick for the favor of bestowing "The Consecrated Rose" on him at that time?**
   Elector Frederick's response was expected to be that he would cull that diseased sheep, Martin Luther, from the clean sheep of the Elector's flock and leave that son of corruption to the judgment of the papal nuncio.

6. **(# F) What was the purpose of the special allowance letters which Miltitz carried with him?**
   Those letters were requesting permission and assistance to pass through the cities with a prisoner, through the cities which were being addressed with those letters,.

7. **(# G) How much greater was Luther's credit than the pope's credit with the German people according to Miltitz's findings?**
   - At least three to one.

8. **(# J & L) What agreement did Miltitz and Luther reach?**
   Luther would stop writing and preaching against the church, providing that his opponents would do the same, all for peace in the church.

9. **(# M) Why was Miltitz in such a hurry to have Luther and the Bishop of Trier, who was also one of the 6 Electors at that time, meet as soon as possible, with the Bishop of Trier to serve as arbitrator?**
   Because it was a top news item that Caesar Maximilian's health was failing rapidly.

10. **(# N) Why did the agreement between Miltitz and Luther have to fail?**
    1. Actually everything was in the hands of our Lord, Jesus Christ (See how you can make Psalm 16 work for you here). The Almighty God had been producing the Reformation Movement in Europe for the good of all people, especially for the good of His Church. 2. The opposition would not have been able to remain silent and let Luther get away with his rebellion against the Pope and the church. It must have been too lucrative of a life for them.

Questions and Answers for Chapter 16

1. **(# A) Why did Dr. Eck choose the city of Leipzig for the debate to take place?**
   Count George, the head of that territory of Saxony, was a strong enemy of Luther throughout his life. Eck thought he would have an advantage for motivating the faculty of the U of Leipzig, and a majority of the common people would be against Luther.

2. **Why did Luther at first remain non-committal about participating in the debate?**
   He had made an agreement with Miltitz that he would not write or preach against the church.

3. (# B) Why was Luther stunned, when he read Eck's actual theses for the debate?

He noticed that Eck's theses were set up against Luther's writings, not against Carlstadt.

4. (# B) Why had Eck actually wanted to debate against Luther rather than against Carlstadt?

In Eck's eyes Luther was a far higher graded debate opponent than Carlstadt.

5. (# C) Why did Luther request of Elector Frederick to let him reverse his promise of silence?

- Because his opponents did not remain silent and the U of Wittenberg would suffer serious damage.

6. (# D) How did Eck publicly explain that he was now regarding Luther as his enemy?

He thought that he knew how to expose Luther as a heretic on points of Luther's opposing Peter's primacy for papal authority, and of Luther's seeming support of John Hus' so called heresy.

7. (# F) What two main points did Luther secretly share with Staupitz?

1. Luther discovered from reading history records that the right and origin of Rome's claim for being the head of the church and worldly powers was not true. 2. He was now beginning to become convinced that the papal office was really the Scripture prophesied Antichrist.

8. Why did Duke George move the debate from the Leipzig U to the Pleissen Castle?

The people attending were too many to be accommodated by space available at the University

9. How had the public interpreted Carlstadt's accident, as the Wittenberg contingent was entering Leipzig?

They considered it as a sort of omen that Carlstadt would lose the debate, and that Luther would be needed.

10. (# H) Name some examples that describe the high level of excitement right before the debate:

Students of Wittenberg were rallying against the students of Leipzig; Bar-room-brawls; a man dying of heart attack; Emser was present to agitate against Luther.

11. Why was Luther against recording the debate speeches?

He just wanted to debate freely. He did not want a panel of judges, most of whom would be R.C.

12. Which two men were behind opposing lecterns at the beginning of the debate?

- Dr. Eck and Dr. Carlstadt

13. (# I) What procedure did Eck request of the judges not to be allowed from the 2nd day on?

- The use of books by the debaters, while they were debating. Carlstadt had been using books for referencing and relied on them, while Eck was more of a "screamer" and known to misquote historic records every now and then.

14. (# J) Why did Luther use Matthew 16:13-19 as sermon text that weekend; and take note of the two main points which Luther was preaching.

The historic pericope called for that Gospel text for that Sunday and what a great fit it was for the occasion. Luther's Part I: The grace of God and the inability of man in spiritual matters, and that Christ would not acknowledge or accept anyone in whom the Father had not produced such action as He did in Peter's case; Part II: The keys were not given to Peter as a person, but were lent to the Church in Peter.

15. How did the Leipzig doctors counter Luther's sermon on Matthew 16:13-19?

They requested Eck to preach four times against Luther's claims, without allowing any rebuttals.

16. (# J) Why did it require courage for Luther to preach that way on that text on that Sunday?

Luther was in hostile territory, and he was preaching contrary to Roman church doctrine.

17. What two noteworthy things happened on the 4th of July during the debate?

1. Luther was allowed to step in and debate instead of Carlstadt. 2. John Tetzel died.

18. May someone in the class read from the last paragraph on p. 111.   *The contents of the paragraph may be further discussed.*

19. (# O) Why did Duke George become extremely upset, when Luther defended a teaching of John Hus?

The war against the John Hus fighters during the previous century had caused many people to get killed and much damage to be rendered, in territory not far from Leipzig. Duke George still regarded the Husites as big enemies and heretics.

20. **(# P) What main position did Luther keep holding throughout the debate?**

    Scripture alone is superior to all other sources for setting forth the full truth.

21. **(# Q) What was the meaning of the water spider illustration which Luther applied to Eck in his final speech?**

    At its own reflection in the water the water spider is frightened. So Eck did not look deeper into Scripture for answers to pertinent questions. Extensive application of the preaching of the cross of Christ seemed to scare him.

22. **On what date did the debate end?**

    - On the 14th of July

23. **What claim did Eck make for himself about the outcome of the debate?**

    He boisterously claimed to have defeated both Carlstadt and Luther. He sang such self-praises in his letter to the papal court. And he down-graded Luther in a letter to Frederick, urging that at least some of Luther's writings should be burned.

24. **How did Amsdorf refer to the whole debate?**

    He wrote to Spalatin: "Simply put, everything Eck wanted was regarded as right and was soon granted, but whatever we asked or sought was rejected as unreasonable and unseemly."

Questions and Answers for Chapter 17

1. **(# A - 1) How did Eck conduct himself after the debate?**

    He repeated his accusations against Luther, claiming that Luther did not acknowledge the authority of the church fathers; 2. That Luther espoused the error of John Hus, and 3. That Luther denied that Christ established the primacy of Peter.

2. **(# A – 2) Luther tells why the Leipzig debate was good for him.**

    It had provided a wider range of respect from people as they learned more about Luther. It led Luther to fight for God's Truth with increasing clarity and decisiveness as battles were taking place.

3. **(# A – 3) As Luther was writing explanations about his theses of the Leipzig debate, what main truth did he insist ever more strongly must be accepted by all Christians?**

    Scripture is the only consistently reliable authority for faith.

4. **(# B - 1) Of what did Eck and Emser now accuse Luther?**

    - Of being guilty of the Hus heresy.

5. **(# B – 4) Why did Luther write the short semi-comical autobiography?**

    It was Luther's clever and light-hearted answer to the charge that Luther was born in Bohemia.

6. **(# B – 6) How did Miltitz and Duke George help to put out the fire under the new attack against Luther by the Bishop of Meisen?**

    When they heard how Luther answered the Bishop of Meisen, and witnessed how the Bishop of Meisen was incensed because of Luther's cynical writing about the slip master, they could not help but burst out with laughter. They considered the whole episode as good entertainment.

7. **(# B – 7) How did Luther answer the condemnation verdict against his theology by the faculties of the universities of Cologne and Louvain (Lyon)?**

    They must use Scripture to substantiate their accusations and not scholastic argumentation.

8. (# B – 8) **Of what did the pamphlet by Prierias in regard to the claimed papal primacy persuade Luther?**
   (Prierias was one of the Pope's main advisers in regard to Bible doctrines.) If this were really the Pope's position, then the Pope must be the Antichrist.

Questions and Answers for Chapter 18

1. (# B) **Augustine von Alveldt of Leipzig claimed that since every earthly organization must have a head, therefore the pope must be the head of the church. What did Luther explain was wrong with this?**
   What really needs to be answered rightly is: Is the Roman papacy genuine or a fraud? Was the Roman Papacy established by divine order or by human order?

2. **How did Luther explain how Christ described His Church?**
   His Church is not of this world. Christianity is a spiritual Church, not a worldly organization. The Head of the Church is Christ, and only Christ (Eph. 4:15-16). All the Apostles were servants and messengers. Luther further proved this with words out of the Third Article of the Apostles' Creed.

3. **To whom did Christ give the power to forgive and to retain sin?**
   Christ gave this power to all the Apostles, (actually to his whole Church) not only to Peter, as the plural form of the personal pronoun **(you)** *in Matthew 18:18 clearly shows.*

4. **According to Luther's opinion why did God allow the papal power to continue on earth?**
   (Note how Luther's position also agrees with the prophecy through the Apostle Paul in 2. Thess. 2:3-4, 9-12.) He held that the Papacy is a cross for the Western church and simply had to be borne, since God had kept allowing it and the worldly governments were not stopping it.

5. **Let's read the second last paragraph on p. 108 to note the three realities which the author of the book saw about Luther's position at that point in his life.**

6. **To whom does the expression "The Laity" refer?**
   - To the nobility and the common people.

7. **Besides continuously instructing people at large with his preaching and pamphlets, and besides actively training next generation pastors with God's Word at the Wittenberg U, to what other group would Luther now turn with the hope of reforming the church?**
   To the German nobility.

Questions and Answers for Chapter 19

1. **Name two members of the German nobility who got their portrait into Graebner's Luther biography?**
   - Ulrich von Hutten and Franz von Sittingen. Both of these were also humanists.

2. (# E) <u>A Point of Information</u>: **About the claimed "Donation of Constantine": Under Rome's own admission (Catholic Encyclopedia V. p. 118) "The Donation of Constantine" is a forged document of Emperor Constantine the Great (272 – 370) to the acclaimed Pope Sylvester I (314-335) by which large privileges and rich possessions were said to have been conferred on the Pope of the Roman Church.**
   (From the pamphlet: "The Split between Roman Catholicism and Christ." P. 8.)

3. (# B) **Why did some nobles offer their castles to Luther as havens of refuge? What had they been thinking might happen?**
   - Elector Frederick the Wise might be forced to stop protecting Luther.

4. **What prompted Frederick the Wise to protect Luther from the Papacy?**
   Frederick the Wise "was careful not to do anything against the truth. And he must have known that Luther's teachings had already sunk deeper roots into the hearts of the people. And if he hadn't noticed, men like Spalatin would

have told him."

5. **(# H) What role was Luther ready to play among the nobles according to his letter to Amsdorf?**

   - The role of a court jester.

6. **(# I) How did Luther advise the nobles to proceed, if and when they might undertake reformation in the country?**

   - With trust in God, and with sincere and humble prayer, rather than with pride of their military and political strength.

7. **(# J) Identify the three walls which the Roman church had erected around itself for purpose of preserving church power?**

   1. The claim that secular powers have absolutely no authority over Rome, rather Rome over them.

   2. No one, except the Pope, was to be allowed to provide final interpretation of Holy Scripture.

   3. No one can summon a council except the pope.

8. **(# K) What basic truth did Luther set forth with the example scenario in the middle of p. 140?**

   - How a small group of Christians, stranded somewhere in a large wilderness, could and would establish officiating leadership among themselves.

9. **(# M) What should take down the 2nd self-protecting wall of the Roman church?**

   Look under "M" in the summary section of this chapter for the answer.

10. **Look up and quote the Bible passage, 2. Cor. 13:8, which teaches the axiom which Luther set forth under #O in the summary section of this chapter.** *"For we cannot do anything against the truth, but only for the truth."* (NIV)

11. **What estimated amount of money was Rome getting out of Germany annually for support of their church operation? Does 40 million dollars sound shocking?**

    *- An estimated 300,000 guilders annually. (See the **(Note)** in chapter 32, p. 59 of this Study Guide, and try to figure out an equivalent sum in current U.S dollars.*

12. **(# Q) Can you recall for what two main purposes Rome claimed the proceeds of indulgence sales and other money-raising schemes and gimmicks were needed?**

    1. Helping to defend Europe against the invading Turks (Mohammedan army); 2. The continuing building of the St. Peter Cathedral in Rome. (But, as Luther explained it - Those proceeds went into a sack without a bottom.

13. **(# R) What mistake might be considered as common to all eight points** *(under "R, a-h)* **that needed reform under Luther's cited list of "26 spiritual improprieties"?**

    - Greed-prompted financial stewardship distortions, coupled with leading the people with the false teaching of buying good favor for oneself from God with monetary payments.

14. **What impression do you feel Luther's "Address to the Nobility" treatise might have given**

    to the nobility? *Many of them might have been encouraged to start cleaning up the spiritual mess.*

    to the common people? *Mixed reactions, but many might have responded, "It's about time."*

    to the clergy of Rome? *Very hostile, or, a major insult.*

15. **When does a church officers ranking system become un-Christian and even abusive?**

    - When it practices and even enforces management laws or procedures that are downright unscriptural; when leaders think themselves to be bosses rather than servants. Note Jesus' teaching in Matthew 20:26-28. We might also read p. 140, paragraph 1, to recognize Luther's basic thinking.

Questions and Answers for Chapter 20

1. **What was the title of the new leader of the Holy Roman Empire in 1520?**
   (See the last line of chapter 20 and the first nine lines of chapter 21 to get the answer.) Charles V of Spain accepted the title, Elected Roman Caesar.

2. **(# A – 1) Name at least two instigators who requested that Luther be served with a papal bull.**
   Dr. Eck, The Fugger Financiers, Cardinal Accolti, Cardinal de Vio, Pope Leo X.

3. **(# A – 3) Why was Elector Frederick so deeply upset?**
   The papal bull was delivered and attempted to be executed in Electoral Saxony, while Frederick himself was away from home, attending the new Caesar's coronation at Aachen.

4. **Can you recall from O.T. history the name of the country into which Israel, which included O.T. believers in Christ, was taken into slavery?**
   Babylon (See 2nd Kings 25:1-21 for a graphic description of that event.)

5. **(# B) How did Luther incorporate that historic truth into the title of one of his special treatises in 1520?**
   "The Babylonian Captivity of the Church"

6. **(# B – 2) What three heresies had the papal power forced on the Christian Church in regard to the celebration of the Lord's Supper?**
   - Provide the answer to this question from the indicated reference "B - 2" under the summary of this chapter.

7. **Why did Luther reduce the number of the Sacraments from 7 to 2 (for a little while from 7 to 3)?** *Because the 3 identification marks for a Sacrament fit only two of these special acts of God.*

8. **(# C – 2 – d) How had Luther been inclined toward the pope when he wrote the treatise, "About the Freedom of a Christian?"**
   He was very friendly and respectful toward the pope.

9. **What two seeming contradictory statements of the Bible did Luther expound under the title "About the Freedom of a Christian?"**
   - 1. Cor. 9:19 and Rom. 13:8. A Christian is free and slave to no one. A Christian is slave to everyone.

10. **(# C - 2 - c) With what description did Luther identify any Christian as a doer of good works?**
    - A good tree producing good fruit, and A good builder builds a good house.

11. **(D) Once Luther had become convinced that it was really the pope who issued the bull against him, what document did he write and send off?**
    "Against the Bull of the Antichrist"

12. **(G) In what context did Luther retract his original 95 Theses?**
    - Because he had not known better at that time, in 1517. Regarding statement number 18 in the list of all of the pope's condemned statements of Luther's 95 Theses (See p. 163 in the book for further information).

13. **On whom else did the pope declare the interdict with his papal bull against heresy?**
    - On Luther and all his followers, no matter how high their position in life. All these were condemned by the pope.

14. **What additional penalties were decreed by the pope in his bull against the Lutheran heresy?**
    They were to be deprived of all honors, dignities, and possessions, and more.

15. **(# E) What event did Luther sponsor at the Elstergate of the Augustinian Monastery in Wittenberg in answer to a previously universally proclaimed decree that all of Luther's books be burned?**
    - The Elstergate Bonfire for the official burning of a copy of the papal bull, and the burning of other false Roman decretals

Questions and Answers for Chapter 21

1. (# A – 2) We would feel stronger if a majority of our Supreme Court could be convinced that the aborting of unborn children is equivalent to murder and would act in response to this basic fact. Why was Luther happy when Charles V would not give support to Luther's appeal for support of the Truth, but instead allowed Luther's book to be burned at Cologne?

    Luther's rejoicing was based on Psalm 118. He concluded, now our people will learn to trust in God all the way and not in princes, or in human strength. Such lessons were also necessary for Reformation success.

2. (# A – 3) If large segments of people decide to rebel against existing government for the sake of the Truth, why should we not participate?

    Governments are established by God for our good. We owe obedience to our government in everything that does not require us to violate his Word.

3. For what two reasons did Elector Frederick want to remain unconnected with Luther's cause?

    1. If it should happen to Luther as had happened to John Hus, he did not want to be blamed for such official injustice.
    2. As head of the province of Electoral Saxony he also did not want to show political favor to Luther, but rather stay personally unconnected.

4. What influenced Caesar Charles V so much that he recommended save escort for Luther to and from Worms?

    He had learned that Luther had too much support among the people, so that he could not be dealt with by having him killed, even if convicted of heresy.

5. What political scheme did Caesar's counselor, Glapio, employ to divert Luther from coming to Worms?

    He was working hard on Elector Frederick's chancellor, Brueck, to gain some small edge in negotiations. But Brueck would not provide him with the slightest concession. The Roman contingent just did not want Luther to appear before the assembled Diet at Worms.

6. (# C – 3) How many days did it take for Luther to arrive at Worms?

    - 15 days

7. What other special ploy did counselor Glapio attempt, to sidetrack Luther from going all the way to Worms and report to the Diet?

    He arranged for Luther to be invited to the Ebernburg Castle, where Franz von Sickingen was having Luther's writings read to him, and from where Hutton had sent his angry and threatening letters to the Roman legates. But that also did not work.

8. (# D – 2) What two questions was Luther asked to answer before the Diet?

    1. Are these your books? 2. Will you recant, or defend these writings of yours?

9. (# D – 3) What was Luther's answer on the first day of his trial before the Diet?

    1. Yes. and 2. I need more time to think how to answer this second question without violating my conscience.

10. Let's read Luther's answer to the same two basic questions on the second day, as he was testifying before the whole assembly of the Diet. *Read 2 paragraphs, beginning with paragraph 5 on p. 175*

11. What was the verdict of Charles V, after Luther had testified before the assembly?

    Charles V was in agreement with the Council of Kostnitz. But Luther would be given save escort back to Wittenberg. However, after that Charles V would come after Luther as a hardened heretic.

12. (# E – 1 & 3) After Caesar was persuaded to extend negotiations with Luther, how many days in all were granted for this purpose?

    - At first six days. Then one more day out of the new allotment of two days.

13. (# E – 4) **How did Luther's departure from Worms differ significantly from his arrival 11 days earlier?**
    There was no fanfare (no parading crowd applauding him) when Luther left.
14. (# E – 5) **What was the surprise ending of the whole Luther episode at Worms?**
    News came back that Luther was attacked on his homeward journey, and no one seemed to know who the attackers were.
15. (# E – 6) **To what illegal document did Caesar Charles V affix his signature on May 26th?**
    The edict of declaring Luther a heretic, known henceforth as "The Edict of Worms"
16. (# E – 6) **Why was this an illegal act?**
    It was dated retroactively to May 8th leaving the impression that the decision was unanimous by all six of the electors at that time.

Question and Answers for Chapter 22

1. (# B) **Why may it have been special for Luther to visit Moehra and Eisenach on his homeward journey?**
    Some of his relatives lived there.
2. **Who had arranged for the kidnapping of Luther and why?**
    Frederick the Wise is thought to have devised this plan, or agreed to it. It makes sense that he may have wanted to provide extended protection for Luther.
3. (# D, E, F, & G) **Can you name some different writings by Luther, while he stayed at the Wartburg?**
    He finished his interpretation of the Magnificat for Prince John. He enlarged the contents of the Postil. He wrote another treatise about the Lord's Supper Bull, which critique he also sent to the Pope. And others.
4. (# I) **What was the most important work of Luther while he was staying at the Wartburg?**
    He translated the New Testament of Holy Scripture from Greek into German.
5. **Let's read the last paragraph on p. 186, starting "The pope would....**
    - to note what made Luther's translation of the New Testament so unique.
6. (# K) **What special project did Archbishop Albrecht again resume in Halle?**
    - The display of his relic collection for purpose of raising money.
7. **How did Luther overtrump the Elector's non-toleration forbiddance in regard to attacking the Archbishop of Mainz?**
    Luther sent an ultimatum letter to the Archbishop, and he let Wittenberg know about it in advance that he would do this.
8. **What two main wrongs did Luther request the Archbishop to correct?**
    1. The sinful relics display must not take place. 2. The incarceration of a pastor, who had gotten married, had to be reversed.
9. **With what action did Luther threaten the Archbishop if he would not reverse his idolatrous activity at Halle, and his imprisoning that certain pastor?**
    Luther would expose and shame the Archbishop.
10. (# M) **What was accomplished with Luther's threatening letter to the Archbishop?**
    The Archbishop complied, completely reversing his actions in regard to these two issues.

Questions and Answers for Chapter 23

1. (B) Why did Dr. Carlstadt cut his visit to Denmark short according to August Graebner?

He saw his chance to take charge of continuing the Reformation.

2. (# B) What was wrong with Carlstadt's interpretation of 1. Timothy 3:2?

He invented a new law out of this passage to the conclusion that no unmarried person may serve in a public spiritual position.

3. (D & E) What was the central problem for the two commissions that had been appointed?

They had dividing opinions and just could not set up a unified solution.

4. (# F) Why did Luther pay a secret visit to Wittenberg?

This evidently was more than only being homesick for his Wittenberg position. He just needed to make an on-site assessment.

5. (# G) What two concerns did Luther express in his letter to Amsdorf?

1. He noted that people had been led to advance too far in the direction of open rebellion. 2. Spalatin had hung on to Luther's writing in regard to the vow for church workers. Luther now demanded publication of that writing, or else an even sharper publication would soon appear.

6. (# G) Give one main reason for Luther's pamphlet, "To All Christians against Insurrection and Rebellion."

"Let your mouth be a mouth of the spirit of Christ in answer to the work of the Antichrist and the devil, but let it not be insurrection.

7. (# H) Name a couple of Carlstadt's premature requirements for his kind of reformation.

Monks and priests should get married. He forced Holy Communion in both kinds. Christian elementary schools were being faced out. The destruction of pictures in churches and other items was being promoted.

8. (# I) Name three of five active leaders who were becoming ever more active. *Zwilling, Pfeifer, Stuebner, Storch, Muenzer, and even Carlstadt.*

9. (# J) Why couldn't Melanchthon and the Elector distinguish correctly and take proper actions against the false prophets which were popping up?

They simply didn't have in-depth understanding the same as Luther in regard to such situations.

10. (# N) Why would Luther no longer obey the Elector, as he decided to come out of hiding?

He just had to get back into the fray of things more directly as he saw the Reformation going forward in the wrong direction.

11. (# O) For what action did Luther rebuke the Elector, as he was coming out of hiding at the Wartburg?

"Now God has listened to your lust and has sent you, free of charge and effort, a whole cross with nails, spears, and scourge. (He meant the cross of the Wittenberg unrest.)

Questions and Answers for Chapter 24

1. (# A) Who was the mystery man, and what was he doing at the Bear's Inn on the outskirts of Jena?

The mystery man was Luther in person. He had stopped for overnight lodging.

2. (# B) What did Luther write to the Elector in reference to Duke George?

" ... Duke George is no match for even a single devil. ... The Father of inexhaustible compassion has made us joyful lords over all devils and death through the gospel and has given us sure confidence ... " Just don't be afraid of Duke George.

3. (# B) Why was the Elector so careful in respect to Duke George of Leipzig?

Duke George was making himself available to Caesar, to lead the imperial army against the nest of Lutherans in Electoral Saxony.

4. (# F) Who were the Zwickau prophets and what were they preaching?

Muenzer, Stuebner and Storch were preaching rebellion and claimed to have been getting such a message directly from God, while they were in the top of a church tower, or in dreams.

5. (# F) How did Luther request of Stuebner and also of Storch to prove their divine calling for their claimed revised reformation plans?

They were to show a sign from God for their revised plan for promoting revolutionary spirit.

6. (# G – 1) How did Luther counsel those who were laying claim to a false religious neutrality?

He explained that people must follow neither Luther nor the pope. But they need to follow Christ. However, if Luther's teachings are the same gospel as Christ's gospel, then they must be careful that they do not throw Christ out.

7. Why couldn't Luther go after the swarming false prophets in other localities right away?

He just had too much work on his desk as well as in his pulpit during that extra busy time of the church year.

8. What had produced rebellious reformation in the city of Erfurt?

A storm had developed, as strong opposition had come about between angry priests and monks on one side, and students and citizens on the other side. This developed after a cantor had been kicked out of choir.

9. How did Luther help out toward subduing the rebellious activity at Erfurt?

- At first with just a letter, a little later that year by personally coming to Erfurt in answer to invitation, and by preaching there several Sundays.

Questions and Answers for Chapter 25

1. **When had Luther translated the New Testament into German?**

While he was at the Wartburg from December, 1521, to the end of March, 1522. After further teamwork reviews in Wittenberg the N.T. was published September 21, 1522.

2. **How was this printed translation received in cities where the Roman Catholic Church was in control?**

It was forbidden to be read, and printed translations were gathered to be taken out of circulation.

3. **(# C) How did the common people in Electoral Saxony receive this translation?**

It was received with joy and enthusiasm. Now the common people could read the Bible themselves. They even started to actively confess the teachings of Holy Scripture. More common people were learning to read. The press had been in motion since 1450.

4. **How far had Luther and his co-workers advanced in translating parts of the Old Testament by the beginning of 1523?** *The five books of Moses and Psalms for sure. The next year, up to the Song of Solomon.*

5. **(# E) With what book did Luther help preachers who didn't know how to write sermons from Bible texts?**

Luther tried to finish the Church Postil, a book which offered short sermons on the gospels. Later Luther also wrote short sermons on the epistles of the church year.

6. **(# F) What was some of the "papal sour dough" in practice that kept being swept out one after another?**

Things like the Corpus Christi Festival, continued distribution of only one kind in the Lord's Supper, the many different private masses, etc.

7. **(# G) Name two of Luther's hymns which were included in the first Lutheran hymnal which consisted of only 8 hymns:**

"Dear Christians, One and All Rejoice ...", "From Depth of Woe ...", "O Lord, Look Down from Heav'n, Behold ...".

8. (# H) **What did Luther urge mayors and city councils to promote as an item of urgent business?**
   The building and maintaining of Christian schools.
9. (# I) **What did Luther say was a good school and what did he regard as a bad school?**
   Schools in which the old languages, especially Greek and Hebrew, were being taught, and where the Bible was being read, were good schools. Other schools, which were usually mainly for purpose of boosting people's personal pride, were not favored by Luther.
10. **Why hadn't it worked out to manage a congregation with a parochial school at Leisnig on the Mulde River?**
    The pastor was not provided a sufficient salary for survival. There also was no financial support for a school.

Questions and Answers for Chapter 26

1. (# A – 1) **What counsel did Luther provide for lower rank people? Name at least two of his writings.**
   1. About human teachings to be avoided. 2. Against the False Positions of the Pope and the Bishops. 3. Christian Congregations Have the Right and Power to Prove All Teachings, and Call Teachers, Install Them, and Put Them out of Office (if necessary).
2. (# A – 2) **How did Luther help troubled nuns?**
   He helped them to escape. He wrote pamphlets in their defense.
3. (# A – 3) **How did Luther ease troubled consciences of monks for whom monastic living had become too big of a struggle?**
   He provided those who desired to escape from sins of monastic life with a sermon, "About Married Life," and with a commentary on 1. Corinthians 7. He also lent a hand with counsel and support to brothers who had quit the monastery.
4. (# A – 4) **How did Luther's persistence for the cause of the Reformation affect some of the soldiers in the imperial army?**
   Many of them turned toward favoring Luther, whereas they had shouted for his death before.
5. **What did Luther think about some of the clergy beginning to get married?**
   He rejoiced with them. In 1523 he even conducted the wedding service, when Link got married.
6. (# B) **What wording in Luther's letter to Kronberg deeply upset Duke George?**
   ... "One of them is especially the waterblister _____. She defies heaven with her big belly." Someone brought a copy to Count George after an anonymous person had inserted George' name into the blank space.
7. (# C – 5) **Luther sharply critiqued the lordship of two different Diets (1526 and 1529), Worms and Nuernberg, for adopting contradictory resolution. Give the name of Luther's writing with which he responded to their sloppy legislating.**
   "Two Imperial Disagreeing and Contradicting Commands against Luther" Luther explained that "It sounds shameful for Caesar and his courts to openly occupy themselves with lying."
8. (# C – 3) **What happened to the knights, Hutton and Sickingen?**
   Both of them got killed in action.
9. (# C – 6) **What semi-secret campaign did legate Cambeggi set into motion?**
   In a special private conference at Regensburg, which lasted 16 days, a minority of dukes of Bavaria and bishops of Southern Germany resolved among themselves to enforce the Edict of Worms.

Questions and Answers for Chapter 27

1. (# A) How had Carlstadt become Pastor of Orlamuende?

   He personally stepped forward within the vacancy of Orlamuende and had himself elected as their pastor. Then he again set into motion his kind of reformation, also taking position against the ministry in Wittenberg.

2. What was wrong about Carlstadt's becoming pastor of Orlamuende?

   He had not been called properly to serve the congregation, but maneuvered himself into that position.

3. (# A – 2) Name several false teachings of Carlstadt:

   See A – 2 – a, b, c, and d in the summary of this chapter for the answer.

4. (# B) How was Muenzer's procedure even worse than Carlstadt's?

   Muenzer preached outright and violent rebellion at Alstedt.

5. (# B – 1) How did Luther counsel the two Electoral Saxon counts *(The Elector and Duke Johann)* with his assessment of the swarmers?

   The Allstedt spirit is evil.

6. (# B – 2) Why did Luther give Carlstadt a gold guilder at Jena?

   He did this to convey that he was very serious in challenging Carlstadt to a debate in Wittenberg, with free escort for Carlstadt to and from Wittenberg. That guilder guarantee also meant that henceforth Luther and Carlstadt were opponents. Carlstadt accepted.

7. How did Luther recognize the Alstedt spirit at Kahla and at Jena?

   At Kahla he found a smashed crucifix in the pulpit, but he preached anyway. At Jena the people showed such an antagonistic spirit, or swarming spirit, that Luther recognized that there was nothing he could do, and so he simply left.

8. (# C) After Carlstadt was ordered out of the country, what special writing did Luther have printed against Carlstadt and his company?

   "Against the Heavenly Prophets about Pictures and the Sacrament"

9. What did Luther anticipate would happen after the Alstedt spirit would have been set into motion?

   "Things would become even worse," meaning rebellion.

Questions and Answers for Chapter 28

1. (# A – 2) Where did rebellion first break out?

   In the Black Forest area between the beginnings, that is, between the springs that started the Rhine and the Danube Rivers.

2. (# A – 3) Note what rebellion looks like closer up by reading the last paragraph on p. 231.

3. (# B) How did Luther answer the indirect invitation to support Swabia's 12 Articles?

   He issued the special writing, "Admonition toward Peace in regard to the 12 Articles of the Farmers' Alliance in Swabia." In this writing Luther first confronted counts, lords, and priests for their tyranny. Then he stated that some of the Articles were fair and right. But their demanding spirit was wrong.

4. (# C) With what special effort did Luther try to stop the rebellion?

   He made an instant trip into Thuringia and started preaching, but all in vain. The rebellious spirit had progressed too far. It seemed to have transformed the masses of people, who were now determined to use force and violence. Luther got out again while he still could.

5. (# D) What writing did Luther issue after that?

   "Against the Murdering and Robbing Rabble of Farmers"

6. (# E & H) How did the rebellion end for Muenzer, Pfeifer, and Carlstadt?

   Pfeifer was killed. Muenzer was executed. Carlstadt survived by the kindness of Luther who interceded for him.

7. (# G) How did things turn out for Luther after suppression of the rebellion?

   Both sides blamed Luther. Luther then issued the writing, "Epistle about the Harsh Pamphlet against the Farmers."

8. (# F) What other special event took place during the Peasant Rebellion?

   Frederick the Wise passed away. His body received Christian burial. Luther preached for the funeral.

Questions and Answers for Chapter 29

1. What was often the sad reality about younger girls being committed to convents as far as age and length of commitment were concerned?

   Girls were simply being victimized because of poverty in the family, or for the sake of convenience for not having to raise them, or by inexcusable guilt feelings, imposed by papal clergy.

2. What were some of the risks in the effort of liberating nuns?

   The liberators were in danger of being caught and prosecuted. The charge would have been, kidnapping, or 'you forced the resident of the convent or monastery to break his/her vow to God.'

3. How did Luther's match-making effort in regard to Katherine von Bora backfire?

   Luther was arranging for her to be courted by other suitors. But it ended up by Kate's eyes being fixed on Luther himself, or on Amsdorf, if Luther would stay unavailable.

4. What may have contributed toward Martin being attracted toward Katherina?

   Martin "may well have been moved by the open honesty of this woman who had been abandoned."

5. Why did Luther rush into marriage after courting Kate for only three months?

   Slander was spreading.

6. How many days after the marriage service of Martin and Kate was the reception dinner held?

   14 days later.

7. When had the law been made that monks and nuns could no longer marry, and those who were married were to consider themseves divorced?

   The year 1075 a.D. (Pope Gregory VII declared all clerical marriages invalid.)

8. What is the story about the wedding rings of Martin and Kate?

   The rings were most likely a later production. See the explanation on pp. 239-240 in the book.

Question and Answers for Chapter 30

1. (# B) Who was Erasmus?

   He was considered by most to be the highest ranking intellectual in philosophy and theology at that time.

2. (# C) What was Erasmus' major problem?

   He had too much personal pride. Should he support that rising Wittenberg monk, oppose him, or just stay away from him?

3. (# B) Why was Martin Luther a problem for Erasmus?

   Luther seemed to be heading for center stage position in theology. What might that do to Erasmus? Erasmus was being confronted by royal and intellectual persons for his opinion about Luther, which confrontations Erasmus just tried to side step.

4. **Why had Leo X given the title "Defender of the Faith" to King Henry VIII?**

   Henry VIII had written a treatise, opposing Luther's treatise, "The Babylonian Captivity of the Church." The Pope gave Henry VIII the title "Defender of the Faith" for this reason. But Luther just shredded Henry VIII's work.

5. **(# D) Why did Henry VIII goad Erasmus into writing against Luther?**

   Henry VIII wanted someone to thrash Luther and expose his theology as false. Who would be better suited for this than the high ranking intellectual Erasmus.

6. **What was Erasmus' major mistake in his "freedom of the Will" diatribe against Luther?**

   Erasmus ignored and even rejected the teaching of God's grace toward totally corrupted sinful mankind. Though he even translated some N.T. books, he did not recognize our biggest need, no Jesus as Savior from all our sins.

7. **(# F)Why was Luther glad that God did not leave it up to him to work out his salvation as a whole or in part?**

   He explained that if it were up to him, when could he ever be sure of having done enough to eliminate God's wrath against sin and accept him worthy for salvation? He then comfortingly quoted from John 10:28 that "No one can snatch them (the Savior's sheep) out of the Savior's hand." Jesus saved all of us by his grace alone through God-given faith in the crucified and risen Christ alone, as taught by Holy Scripture alone.

Questions and Answers for Chapter 31

1. **By what outward means did God cause his Gospel to spread to many cities, territories, and countries?**

   By having let the printing press be invented about 75 years earlier, and having let it be used for massive distribution of His Word. This, too, had happened only by our God's guiding of history and bestowing talents on individuals. (Check out Proverbs 21:1)

2. **By what spiritual means did the whole Reformation movement happen in Luther's life time?**

   By the testimony of the Gospel of Christ with spoken and printed Word.

3. **(# C) What did God not allow Luther to apply in the spreading of the Gospel?**

   God did not allow Luther to compromise His Word for any situation.

4. **(# F) In what connection did Luther both love and lament when he heard about the death of Staupitz?**

   Love motivated him when he recalled how this dear teacher was used to start opening his eyes for understanding the Gospel of Christ. He lamented the death of Staupitz's when he recalled how he did not want to stay in the heat of the battle for the truth, but instead moved away to another location for the last two years of his life.

5. **How was the death of Voes and Esch different than the death of Staupitz?**

   Voes and Esch were killed because of their preaching the Gospel of Christ. Their testimony continued to sound out after they were martyred, as Luther also noted with the memorial hymn he wrote about them.

Questions and Answers for Chapter 32

1. **For what purpose had the home of Martin Luther served before the Elector gave it to him?**

   It had been the Augustinian Monastery of Wittenberg, providing housing and humble living quarters for monks as they were being trained for the work of the ministry.

2. **Who was the better gardener, Martin or Kate?**

   - Kate for sure. She must have had more patience, skill, and dedication for manual work around the house, on the land, and on behalf of the estate.

3. (# C) **How high was the salary of Luther before and after his marriage?**

   Just how low it was before Luther's marriage I do not know. I learned that he received $0.00 when he was first transferred to Wittenberg. Was his salary adjusted when he received his doctor title? Possibly. His salary was raised by the Elector to 200 guilders (annually, I assume) right after their marriage. But Luther also received help for repairing and maintaining the building now and then from the city council.

4. **What was the probable cause for Luther's near death in 1527?**

   - Most likely extremely high blood pressure. It could also have been infection via the invading plague.

5. **Name Martin and Kate's first three children:**

   Johannes; Elizabeth, who died less than a year after her birth; and Magdalena, who died at the age of 12.

6. (# F) **Name some of the extra duties which occupied Luther, besides lecturing and preaching for Bugenhagen, when Bugenhagen had been called to help for organizational work elsewhere.**

   Luther kept working on translating other books of the Bible and expanding the Postil besides all his preaching.

Questions and Answers for Chapter 33

1. (# A) **How were Luther and the new Elector getting along with each other?**

   They were getting along very well, even better than Luther got along with Frederick the Wise, which had been good.

2. (# B) **What special project did the Elector assign to Luther?**

   Luther was directed to design a new Sunday worship service in the German language.

3. **For how many worship services did Luther serve per week?**

   - At least nine. Three Sunday services, one morning service per day from Monday to Friday, and one Saturday evening service.

4. **In what way was exorcism connected with baptism in the church services at Wittenberg in those days?**

   Apparently a special exorcism rite was attached in the administering of baptism.

5. **Is there still a connection between baptism and exorcism today when a baptism is being administered?**

   In Acts 26:18 Scriptures inform us of a part of the Apostle Paul's call which he provided as testimony with the words, "I am sending you to them to open their eyes and turn them from darkness to light and from the power of Satan to God." Every person who is born in sin finds himself under the power of Satan. When a person is being baptized, control by Satan is taken away. In that sense baptism has set us free. Satan's control over our lives has been eliminated. We belong to our God who created us. (Psalm 100:3 might be applied.)

Questions and Answers for Chapter 34

1. **Why was it necessary to make church visitations to the different congregations at that time?**

   Parishes were in terrible spiritual condition. Financial support for pastors was low. A large number of commoners had little respect for ministerial servants in their midst. Before any corrections could be tried, they needed to make a more accurate assessment of the situation.

2. **What information did the Elector and Luther seek to obtain by visiting the congregations?**

   Did the people and their pastors understand and use the Gospel of Christ? Did they know any of the other teachings in the Bible? Were they even able to afford buying a N.T.? To what extend were sextons (general janitors and managers of church properties) able to help? etc.

3. **What was the special writing by Luther with which the congregations were to acquaint themselves and would possibly adopt the same for use in their congregations?**

    "The German Mass and Order for Divine Service Undertaken at Wittenberg."

4. **(# E) How many were on Luther's team when he was also requested to serve as a visitor in 1528?**

    - Five persons; Two theologians and three other visitors.

5. **(# F) What abominable findings did Luther report?**

    "Things are terrible within congregations in that the farmers learn nothing, know nothing, pray nothing, and do nothing except abusing their freedom, do no confession, no communion attendance. They behave as though they had been completely set free from religion."

6. **(# F) Name the two counter measures which were begun to be put into practice.**

    1. No one would be allowed to the Sacrament who could not at least say the 10 Commandments, the Confession of Faith, and the Lord's Prayer. 2. The sextons were to be held responsible to have the children at least memorize the 10 Commandments, the Creed, and the Lord's Prayer.

7. **(# G) Why did Luther have to be recalled from visiting congregations to lecturing in the classroom?**

    Students were leaving the U, due to Luther's and Melanchthon's continuing absence.

Questions and Answers for Chapter 35

1. **How was the new Gospel freedom being abused by common people?**

    They hardly knew anything about Christ's teachings, especially in the villages. Parish lords (Pastors) in many instances were unskilled and neglectful.

2. **(# B) For how many years, before the Catechism was printed had Luther been occupying himself to determine what basic knowledge common people should have?**

    - At least since 1520, and now it was the year 1528.

3. **(# C) Which Catechism was the first to come off the press?**

    - The Large Catechism, which was urged to be used faithfully (especially by pastors s and teacher) and not soon be thrown into a corner after reading it once, or even twice. A secret alliance with complacency and boredom just had to be knocked out.

4. **(# D) What were some of the phrases or parts which were being added in revised addition during the next two years?**

    The Address to the Lord's Prayer; How Can Eating and Drinking Do Such Great Thing; and What Does This Mean?; Directive for Confession; Office of the Keys; and Christian Questions.

5. **With what other description was the Catechism of Luther referred to in the Luther biography?**

    "Luther's Small Catechism is second only to the Bible," and even "The Layity Bible."

Questions and Answers for Chapter 36

1. **(# A, B & N) Name three places or territories where Gospel witnesses were being martyred.**

    Nine martyrs at Bamberg, the two martyrs in the Netherlands; After the Peasants War, the Oschatz people in and near Leipzig; There was continued threatening by Charles V, by Count George, and others; the preacher at Halle, et al.

2. (# E) **In what way had Luther misjudged Henry VIII and Duke George?**

   He had thought that they were beginning to believe the Gospel, but was disappointed when, with a couple verbal kicks in his rear, he found out otherwise.

3. (# F) **In what way had Duke George misjudged Luther after he read the pamphlet, "Whether Soldiers Can also Be Saints."**

   He spoke words of praise for the man who wrote that wonderful pamphlet until he found out that Martin Luther was that man.

4. (# H & I) **What huge concession did the first Diet of Speyer make toward the Evangelicals?**

   The heads of governments were to determine which religion was to be practiced in their territory.

5. (# J) **What actually happened to the city of Rome in 1527?**

   Rome was sacked by a German mercenary army.

6. (# N) **Why did Elector Joachim of Brandenburg have his wife, Elizabeth, imprisoned?**

   She had asked for and received the Lord's Supper in both kinds, in accordance with the words of Institution by Christ.

7. **Why had Caesar Charles V again become a very dangerous enemy against the Gospel truth?**

   He had made peace with the pope again and had set his sight toward "The extermination of the Lutheran sect", as he stated it.

8. (# P) **With what scam did Otto von Pack deceive Count Philip and also Elector John?**

   He claimed that an alliance had been formed against the Evangelical leaders. He even had forged a sealed document with many details which looked genuine. With this scam he first persuaded Philip of Hessen, and he, in turn, informed Elector John, and some extensive war preparations were being undertaken.

9. (# P) **What was Luther's advice, when he was asked, and which then prevented the outbreak of a war against Catholicism?**

   Be patient, wait out any such attack, and call on Caesar for protection.

Questions and Answers for Chapter 37

1. (# B) **With what message had Luther urged all Germans in 1528 with his writing, "Concerning the War against the Turks?"**

   Fight for Caesar against the Turk. The Turk is the major worldly threat against all Christendom.

2. (# A & C) **What was the first convention action of the second Diet at Speyer in 1529?**

   A motion was adopted to rescind the adopted motion three years earlier at Speyer that heads of government should determine the religion to be practiced in their territories.

3. (# E) **With what two reaction did the Evangelicals respond to the newly adopted resolution at Speyer?**

   The first reaction was a strong protest. When that failed, they forged a document of appeal. (See p. 274) for a few more details.)

4. (# F) **What else did the Evangelicals do in response to the newly adopted resolution at Speyer?**

   They formed an alliance to stand united and to defend themselves jointly, should any of them be attacked.

5. (# G) **What special hymn did Luther write and compose during those threatening days?**

   "A Mighty Fortress Is Our God."

Questions and Answers for Chapter 38

Note: Luther's phrase, "Frau Hulda," referring to human reason as an enemy of God. In his commentary of the 1st Commandment Luther called Hulda a devil. He also referred to Hulda as a witch. (Luther's Saemmtliche Schriften, Vol III, columns 1150 and 1156)

1. (# A) Name two bad consequences that would result, if human reason were allowed to interpret Scripture.
   1. Human reason, when taking charge, will lead to the denial of Christ being God. 2. As it continues to want to stay in control, soon no articles of faith would be left.

2. (# B) With what other gospel preacher did Luther compare Carlstadt?
   - With Zwingli.

3. (See the first 14 of the Marburg Articles on pp. 290-291) In what respect were Luther's and Zwingli's teachings similar (though not the same) according to the Marburg Articles?
   The Trinity, the Person of Christ, Original Sin, Faith, Righteousness, the Word of God, Baptism, Good Works, Confession, the Government, Ceremonies, Infant Baptism, Holy Communion.

4. (# D, E, & F) In what respect was Luther opposed to Zwingli's teachings?
   - In respect to human reason verses faith (including about the Lord's Supper, Baptism, Original Sin.). Zwingli kept insisting that the word for "is" should be translated "signifies" in the words of our Savior's institution of the Lord's Supper.

5. (# I) On what two false premises did Luther explain that the Swiss reformers based their denial of the real presence of Christ's body and blood in Holy Communion?
   1. This doctrine was a very clumsy thing in light of reason. 2. They believed that it was unnecessary for Christ's body and blood to be in the bread and wine.

6. (# O – 3) Give several good results which Luther thought could come about from his writing, "Confession about the Supper of Christ."
   1. Some students reading it would be informed correctly. 2. The weaker Christians could be strengthened and preserved. 3. Luther would have left a clear witness for all.

7. (# P) Where did Carlstadt finally find a home?
   - With the Swiss reformers.

Questions and Answers for Chapter 39

1. (# A) Why was Luther against forming a political alliance which would include cities of South Germany?
   He informed the Elector that such an alliance would also include alliance with false teachings.

2. (# D) In what regard did the Wittenberg theologians consider Philip of Hessia and Zwingli as being like two birds of the same feather?
   They both were basically political minded and also applied such procedure in the use of theology.

3. (# F) Who were the main debaters at the Marburg Colloquy?
   - Luther facing Zwingli and Oecolampad. The other Wittenbergers spoke very seldom.

4. (# F – 2) From which four words did Luther never want to be separated during the debate?
   From the words, "This is my body."

5. (# F – 3) Which two false teachings about the Lord's Supper did the Swiss reformers refuse to let go?
   - The false interpretation of John 6:63, and actually the doctrines of Christ's omnipresence and omnipotence.

6. **(# G) In regard to what use of reason did Luther yield absolutely nothing in the Marburg Colloquy?**
   - The use of human logic for making the real presence of Christ's body and blood in the Lord's Supper more acceptable for staying in tune with Mrs. Hulda.
7. **How many persons signed the Marburg Articles? Can you discern their names from their signatures?**
   - Ten persons. I feel the second question for these professionals deserves a "Yes" answer.
8. **(# I) For what reason could Luther not shake hands with the Swiss reformers at the end of the debate?**
   *Luther's conscience, based on God's Word, evidently did not allow him to extend the hand of Christian fellowship. Luther knew that the Holy Spirit is only one Spirit, not divided into two opinions. (See Ephesians 4:1-4. (Review **Essays on Church Fellowhip**, pp. 309-335 by E.E.Kowalke, if time permits.)*
9. **(# J) In what way did the reports at home base of the two opposing sides at Marburg differ?**
   The Swiss reformers did some boasting back at home, like Dr. Eck had done after the Leipzig debate. Luther reported calmly from his pulpit in Wittenberg that not brotherly, but charitable friendly unity prevailed, except for one somewhat heated outbreak.

Questions and Answers for Chapter 40

1. **(# A) What was Luther's main objection against forming an armed alliance against Caesar Charles V?**
   Membership for the proposed alliance, including the southern cities of Germany, was contingent upon signing the confession of the Schwabach Articles, as Luther had drawn them up during the return trip from Marburg. But Luther's main objection remained that Charles V was their God-instituted head of government.
2. **(# B) In what other way did Luther also support Caesar, though Caesar was bent on destroying Luther?**
   Luther had written a strong sermon to all Germans to support the emperor against the Turkish army, which was a main enemy against all Christendom.
3. **Who is meant with the phrase on p. 295, "The hand which would remain free."**
   Caesar Charles V was meant.
4. **What is meant with the phrase , "What kind of weather he would provide."**
   Our God ,who directs the unfolding of world history, was meant.
5. **(# D) How did the Elector John Frederick begin to prepare for the Imperial Diet at Augsburg?**
   Right after he had received the invitation he sent a message to all those counts, who were his spiritual brothers, requesting that they attend the Diet. 2. He requested of the Wittenberg theologians to set up clearly stated articles for presenting the Wittenberg position before the Diet, and that they submit these articles to the Elector by March 18, 1530.
6. **(# F) Where were Coburg and Augsburg located in relation to Berlin and Wittenberg?**
   Coburg was about half way between Wittenberg and Augsburg, in a south by southwestern direction from Berlin, which is in a more northern location of Germany. (See the map on p. 91)
7. **(# F) Why did the Elector leave Luther at the Coburg?**
   Luther was regarded a national criminal by most government leaders as well as by the Roman Church. He had not been invited to Augsburg. The Elector wanted to keep Luther as close as possible, but also under protection.
8. **(# G) For what purpose did Luther want to build three shrines, while he would stay at the Coburg?**
   He wanted to follow a general agenda for his forthcoming studies. He wanted a shrine for the prophets, another for the Psalms and a third for Aesop. He wanted to be translating and interpreting the Prophets and Psalms. A shrine for Aesop meant that he considered those fables helpful for purpose of interpreting.
9. **(# H) With what kingdom did Luther compare the lordships at Augsburg?**
   - The kingdom of the birds.

10. (# I) **What task did Luther undertake in regard to the O.T. while he was at the Coburg?**

He roughly translated nearly all of the O.T.

11. (# J) **Why had Luther dedicated one of his imaginary shrines to Aesop?**

He translated these fables into German, because he believed a person could find in them the best teachings, warnings, and instructions with very simple words, for anyone who knows how to use them.

12. (# K) **What special advice did Luther give to the spiritual lordships assembled at Augsburg?**

He wrote a sharp "Admonitions to the Spiritual Leaders Gathered at Augsburg for the Imperial Diet."

13. (# L & I) **Why did Luther insert the word "alone" into his translation of Romans 3:28?**

He explained that he did this, because translation out of Greek language mindset calls for it.

14. (# L – 2) **How did Luther compare his translating skill with the Apostle Paul as Paul supplied his qualifications for being a true Apostle?**

Luther's translation skills were simply far superior to the skills of the translators for the Roman church. And the Roman church had dared to blame Luther for having contained many translation mistakes in translating the N.T, as they were judging him on the basis of the Vulgate which had many mistakes. When Luther saw mistakes in the Vulgate, he would not honor them by copying such false translation in the Latin version of St. Jerome.

15. (# M) **Why did Luther consider it very important that children receive a good education?**

He said that this is important and necessary. For Jesus promised that he and his gospel will be with us until the end of time, but through whom if not through our children? For this you need schools, etc.

16. (# N, O & P) **With what other projects did Luther occupy himself during his five months and 20 days' stay at the Coburg?**

- With translating Holy Scripture, with writings on different topics, with writing many official and many personal letters, with time for in-depth prayers, with time for people who came to visit him, with the news that his father had died, with time for recuperating from exhaustion and even from deep depression, and more.

17. **With what Bible reference might "God's rod and staff in his hand" be compared, and how might this be further understood?**

Would Moses before Pharaoh, or at the Red Sea, or Joshua at the Jordan be a fit (or Psalm 23:4)?

18. (# R) **What was the other question for which the Elector was asking Luther to give his answer?**

How should the Evangelicals respond to Caesar's request that they do no preaching in Augsburg while they were awaiting his delayed arrival? Luther responded that they appeal to him to make uniform allowance for both sides. If that would not be granted, then just obey him.

19. (# T) **Why did the Elector and Philip of Hessia refuse to kneel, when Campegio seized the opportunity and pronounced a blessing on the procession?**

They refused to participate in that kind of fellowship. They also would not take off their hats in the cathedral, when worship service was being conducted.

20. (# U) **What was the two way blockade of letter writing about?**

Luther's co-workers at Augsburg had stopped writing to Luther, no longer passing on information how things were coming along. Finally Luther in deep disappointment informed them that he too would now stop writing to them.

21. (# V) **Once the blockade was lifted, of what did Luther accuse and scold Melanchthon?**

- In regard to his self-imposed rational philosophical depression.

22. (# X) **When was the confession of the Evangelicals read before the assembled royalties at Augsburg, and how long did the reading last?**

- Saturday, June 25, 1530, from 3:00 to 5:00 p.m.

23. (# Z) **Why did Luther compare the Archbishop of Mainz with Gamaliel in his special letter to the Archbishop?**
Though Gamaliel was on the side of the opposition, against Christ and the Apostles, he did some excellent counseling (Acts 5:34-40). Archbishop Albrecht had also given some good advice. Luther wrote to the Archbishop and asked him to continue advising toward peace.

24. (# AA) **Why did the refutation, which Charles V had ordered, turn out to be such a sham?**
Charles V considered the first draft of the refutation an abominable writing. After it had been re-written several times, Charles V still seemed ashamed to give a copy of it to the Evangelicals. The Roman Catholic theologians just could not justify their position with the use of Scripture."

25. (# CC) **What was Luther's sharp warning while the participants of the arbitration commission were haggling?**
Do not start compromising, lest you will lose the gospel. You just cannot unify the pope with Luther.

26. (# CC) **What only way did Luther figure the discussion of the appointed commission, if continued, could end?**
The gospel would again be shackled, or imprisoned.

27. (# DD) **What was happening to Melanchthon during those extended negotiations?**
He was weakening and beginning to imagine that he could persuade the other side by giving in a little.

28. (# EE) **Why was Caesar's closure, which the Evangelicals refused to accept, irrational?**
It stood opposed to the Gospel witness, and he kept holding that position without acceptable proof.

29. (# GG) **Which of the Torgau-based Saxon royalties arrived first at the Coburg on their homeward journey?**
- Prince John.

30. (# HH) **Let's read the summary of Luther's comforting letter to the Elector as printed on p. 311:**

31. (# JJ) **How did Luther gently chastise Melanchthon at Altenburg on their homeward journey?**
He took the quill right out of his hand and reminded him that God also can be served by celebrating and resting.

Questions and Answers for Chapter 41

1. **What deadline had Caesar issued for the Evangelicals?**
By April 15, 1531 he wanted the Lutherans to have returned to the Roman Catholic fold and to have restored all formerly confiscated properties.

2. (# B & C) **What did the Evangelicals feel obligated to do shortly after the Diet of Augsburg?**
They needed to organize themselves as an alliance so that they could stand unified in support of one another, if any of them should come under attack.

3. (# D) **State three main points Luther made in his editorials for German citizens.**
1. We prayed for peace, not war. 2. We shall speak a blessing on them, "Just as holy as you are on God's behalf, so great may be the type of fortune and victory God will grant you." 3. Those who decide to defend themselves against the blood-thirsty papists are justified in doing so.

4. (# E) **Why could Caesar not enforce the deadline he had given?**
The 250,000 strong Turkish army was at the eastern boundary of the Empire. Charles V needed the Germans to help defend the Empire.

5. (# F) **On what date was a peaceful solution reached for the Holy Roman Empire?**
On June 23, 1531 at Nuernberg.

6. (# G) **What caused Sultan Pasha to retreat from Vienna with his army?**
A German army of 80,000 had succeeded to hold Sultan Pasha's forces at bay at Vienna. When the Sultan realized

125

that the Roman Empire stayed united, he had no other recourse but to retreat.

7. (# H) Can you still distinguish between the three "Fredericks" in Electoral Saxony

    (with descriptive names and years in office? Otherwise review the end of chapter 27 in the Study Guide.)

8. (# I) How did internal peaceful conditions in the Empire favor the spread of the Reformation?

    A substantial growth was happening. New territories and cities started joining the Reformation Movements.

9. Read the last paragraph of this chapter and see, if you can recognize a connection with at least some ancestors of WELS.

    Ancestors of many WELS members hailed from Pommern - Pommerania, in north-east Germany.

Questions and Answers for Chapter 42

1. (# B) What did Cardinal Vergerius want to accomplish with his visit to Wittenberg?

    He was exploring different possibilities for the location of a coming church council.

2. What special change in the life of Cardinal Vergerius happened by 1542?

    He became a Lutheran.

3. (# C) Why were King Franz of France and Henry VIII of England not accepted into the Smalcald League?

    They had wanted to join only for political and personal reasons.

Questions and Answers for Chapter 43

1. (# A) Which four southern cities wanted to be taken in as members by the Lutherans?

    - Strassburg, Constance, Memmingen, and Lindau.

2. (# B) What caused the early death of Zwingli?

    He was killed in a Swiss internal war near Zurich.

3. (# D & E) On what point of doctrine did Luther want to be very clear in the discussions with the theologians of the southern cities?

    On the reception of the Lord's body and blood by his guests at the altar. "The ungodly also receive the very same body of Christ in the celebration of the Lord's Supper."

4. On what date did Bucer and his companions reach agreement with the Lutheran theologians?

    On Ascension Day May 24, 1536 at Wittenberg.

5. (# F) How did Luther explain in friendly conversation that his preaching was better than Bucer's with which Bucer had agreed?

    Bucer was using a higher – more intellectual - level of speech while preaching. In that sense he seemed to be preaching more over the heads of his listeners. On the other hand, Luther was reaching more into the lives of common people, like into a mother nursing her child, etc.

Questions and Answers for Chapter 44

1. (# A – 1) What was one of Pope Paul III's goals for the proposed Council of Mantua for May, 1537?

    - "The extirpation of the poisonous Lutheran heresy."

2. (# A – 2, 3, & 4) Why did Elector John want Luther to draw up a special set of articles during the last months of 1536?

    He directed Luther to put his teachings into articles to be submitted to the other Wittenberg theologians for approval or correction. Such a confession, if needed, was to be ready for submission to the proposed Church Council at Mantua.

3. (# B) In regard to which part(s) of his articles did Luther know in advance that the Roman Catholic Church would never agree?

- *To portions of part II and to part III.*

4. **(# D) When and where did about 40 Lutheran theologians meet to discuss and support Luther's teachings?**

    - *At Smalcald in February, 1537.*

5. **(# E) What became a bigger concern for the assembly after they arrived at Smalcald?**

    - *The rapidly declining health of Luther.*

6. **(# F) For what purpose did Bucer and Wolfhart make the special trip to Gotha?**

    They had heard that Luther was moved there, and they wanted to stay in contact with him, who had promised that he would do for them what he could to assist the cause of these southern cities. Indirectly he had kept supporting them, all of which seemed to be regretted only a few years later.

7. **(# G) Why did the Evangelicals finally feel compelled to decline the attending at the proposed Council of Mantua?**

    - *Because Lutherans had already been declared condemned without having received a hearing.*

8. **(# H) Why were the Smalcald Articles adopted, and were also included as one of the main confessional writings of the Lutheran Church?**

    - *Because they were based directly on Holy Scripture. They also were signed by all those who attended. Only Melanchthon had some reservation.*

9. **(# I) What special treatise by Melanchthon was also somewhat adopted by the Reformation theologians?**

    - *The tract about "The Primacy of the Pope."*

Questions and Answers for Chapter 45

1. **(# A – 1) What other special religious alliance had been formed in Germany?**

    A counter-reformation alliance was started by Count George of Saxony, Count Heinrich von Wolfenbuettel, and Count Erich von Kalenberg.

2. **(# A – 2 & 3) Why could this newly formed alliance not start a war against the reformation alliance?**

    1. The Turk was on the move again. 2. Charles V would not favor such a move at that time.

3. **(# A) What special happening on April 17, 1539, served as very favorable for the Reformation Movement?**

    - *The death of Duke George.*

4. **(# B) In respect to whom was the homage celebration conducted on the Eve before Pentecost?**

    It was conducted in respect to Heinrich, the brother of George. He was being installed as legal heir of the throne of secular Saxony.

5. **(# B – 1) What other area of Germany also changed from Catholic to Evangelical?**

    The dukedom of Kalenberg.

6. **(# B – 2) What purpose had Charles V wanted the meeting at Hagenau to serve?**

    - *To bring about a renewed Christian equality.*

7. **(# D) Why could a reconciliation between Catholicism and the Reformation Movement never happen?**

    The Romanist would never give up the Roman Mass, as Luther had forewarned after he had written the Smalcald Articles, and, of course, the Almighty God was also directing this aspect of the unfolding of world history.

8. **(# B – 2) Though there could be no unity between the Catholics and the Lutherans, what favorable result did come out of the Hagenau Diet?**

    Charles V did allow for Christian equality in religion (In regard to which he later also again changed his mind, like the Pharaoh in Egypt had kept on doing).

9. **(# E) What other renewed policy had favorably served the Reformation Movement?**

The religious peace, which had been established at Nuernberg in 1532, was re-confirmed by Caesar.

10. (# F) However, what new papal announcement posed the next big threat for the reformation movement?
The Pope announced that a Church Council would be held at Trent in 1545, which the Evangelicals were expected to attend.

Questions and Answers for Chapter 46

1. (# B) What was Luther's preferred work with which he loved to occupy himself?
- *Translating and Interpreting Holy Scripture.*

2. (# B - 2) For which book of the Bible did Luther say he had special love, calling it even his Kate of Bora?
- *Galatians*

3. (# B) Name one of the Psalms which were among Luther's favorites.
Psalm 118, Psalm 110, actually all of them.

4. Can you say why Luther favored such a Psalm?
Psalm 118 helped him overcome fear for high earthly powers and to trust in God instead. Ps. 110 he really liked for the central statement, "You are a priest forever in the order of Melchizedek," and for providing the quintessence of the history of the Church amidst the whole history of this world.

5. (# C - 2) In what year was the translation of the whole Bible into German first printed?
- *In the year 1534*

6. (D) Can you name a couple of hymns which were written by Luther?
See chapter 25, answer # 7; also: "From Heav'n above ... ," A Mighty Fortress .... ," "We now Implore God, the Holy Ghost (vss 2-3) ... ," "Isaiah, Mighty ... ," etc.

7. What warning did Luther give in regard to hymn writing?
"Many false masters do hymns now compose. Beware and discern them and rightly dispose." - False teaching can easily creep into rhymes and then begin to spread false leaven into wider areas.

8. (# E) What did Luther call the highest abomination of the papacy?
The Mass (the mass sacrifice, hidden mass, and other corruptions)

9. (# F) To whom was Luther referring when he spoke about religious swarmers? -
At times he was referring to all who sneak into the fold through the back door; but then especially to such as Zwilling, Pfeifer, Stuebner, Storch, Muenzer, even Carlstadt, Zwingli, and other Swiss reformers.

10. (G) Why did Luther write against the Jews?
- *Because they rejected Christ, who had been born out of their own midst, when they were rated as central nation of God.*

11. How many opponents of Luther can you name?
The popes, the Zwinglians, the Turks, the two Dr. Ecks and others in the Roman curia, Charles V, Count George plus numerous other counts, cardinals, bishops, and priests, Henry VIII, Erasmus, etc.

12. (# H) In what way was Luther hurt by Agricola?
They used to be very good friends. But then Agricola's type of teaching changed to the form of antinomianism, that is, the extreme minimizing of God's law in preaching. Agricola even misrepresented Luther when he was challenged to debate about the topic.

13. (# K – 1) Where was Justus Jonas installed as preacher?
He was installed in Halle.

14. (# K – 1 – a) Why did Archbishop Albrecht feel obligated to move out of one of his favorite city?

He needed to move out of Halle, because Luther had exposed his display of relics as a form of practicing idolatry. Local Lutheran preachers after that made the Archbishop feel uncomfortable. In fact, the Archbishop himself had become a more ardent student of the Greek New Testament.

15. (# L – 3) What had Luther instructed his wife to do, after life in Wittenberg had become quite godless?

He wrote that she should sell all their belongings and then come and join him. He did not want to live in Wittenberg any longer.

16. (# L – 4) What did the Elector and Luther's colleagues, together with the city council of Wittenberg, do to get him to come back?

They sent the mayor and some of his colleagues after him to convince him to come back. They promised that they would help him clean up that upswing of ungodliness.

17. (# M) Why did Luther not want to be grouped with the Zwinglians under all the new so-called sects?

- Because of their denial of the body and blood in the Lord's Supper. Luther had not separated himself from the Roman church. All along he had still wanted a hearing in a church council, after the pope had dared to excommunicate him. Such was not the case with Zwingli.

18. (# O) What was Luther's special threefold advice for correctly studying theology?

Oratio! Meditatio! Tentatio!

19. (# K – 4) How might we explain what is wrong with basic teaching and practice of Anabaptists?

Infant baptism in the name of the Triune God is Scriptural. Re-baptism of adults, based on their own reasoning, is wrong. Those who do so are not understanding the teaching of God's grace rightly; plus other false teachings.

20. (# L – 5) How ought we to apply Luther's position on usury today?

(See the paragraph on p. 359) In line with the 7th Commandment and the way Jesus obeyed it, usury is wrong. But let us also interpret various references to Christian financial stewardship properly; and what about Matthew 26:11?

21. Might we today assess Melanchthon's double role differently than the way the late Prof. Graebner assessed it?

1. Remember Luther's consistent stand against making doctrinal compromises. 2. Then let us lovingly continue to take a firm stand against all hypocritical compromising in respect to Bible doctrines and practice. 3. Let us be careful not to sidestep God's forewarning in Romans 1:18-2:4. 4. Let us remember Romans 12:19ff, and pray Psalms 51 and 32 from the heart. But let us also keep in mind the historic Lutheran position as expressed by F. Bente in the Historical Introduction to the Symbolical Books of the Triglotta. Finally, let us humbly but also firmly keep in mind and apply the Bible doctrines about Church Fellowship, and why our gracious God wants us to maintain doctrinal position in respect to so much generic religion all around us.

Questions and Answers for Chapter 47

1. (# B & H) Name the six children of Martin and Kate Luther.

Johannes, Elizabeth, Magdalena, Martin, Paul, and Margareta.

2. (# A) What was the approximate annual income for Luther during his last year in life?

- $32,830.00 (according to the 2015 value of the U.S. dollar)

3. Name some other valuables which Luther possessed.

- Chalices, rings, chains, which Luther estimated to be worth about 1,000 guilders, equivalent to about

$131,320.00 according to the 2015 value of the U.S. dollar.

4. (# C) What is the Luther House Postil?

Shorter sermons that Luther would preach at home, much of which had its beginning in the years 1532-1534, when Luther in sickly condition was restricted to spend more time at home.

5. What were some of Luther's favorite food items?

- Pork and sausage.

6. What is the title of the book in which some of the mealtime conversation by Luther was being preserved?

- "Luther's Table Talks."

7. How many health problems in Luther's life can you recall?

- Heart problems, high blood pressure, kidney stone attacks, deep depressions, headaches, diarrhea, boils, an opening in his leg, apparently for draining.

8. What had been some of Kate's illnesses?

- Intermittent fever, miscarriage and near death after effects, infestations from plagues that would move through towns and cities.

9. When did Luther's parents die?

- His father in 1530 while he was at the Coburg, his mother a year later.

10. What kind of personal relationship did Martin and Kate have with each other?

They loved each other and got along well with each other. Their love for each either seemed to increase from year to year all the way from the time when they were married.

11. For converting money values of that time into U.S dollars in 2015, refer to p. 60 in this compendium, chapter 32, "C", about the value of a 16th century Rhenish guilder according to Ernst Schwiebert's "Luther and His Times."

Questions and Answers for Chapter 48

1. (# A) What special advice did Luther give to his friend, Paul Eber, during Luther's last birthday celebration?

"Your name is Paul. I therefore now admonish you, that following Paul's example, you are to make every effort to firmly preserve and defend the teaching which he proclaimed."

2. (# B) For what purpose did Luther and some of his friends and family members travel to Mansfeld several times during the winter of 1545-1546?

- To help settle a long-time dispute between the counts of Mansfeld.

3. (# C & D) Why had Luther posted that special note on the door to his study about an examination of the Wittenberg professors?

"The professors should be examined about the Lord's Supper." In this context he issued a warning about the light of reason against faith as Luther stated in his last sermon at Wittenberg.

4. (# F) On what date was the reconciliation between the counts of Mansfeld completed?

- February 17, 1546.

5. (# E) How often did Martin write letters to his Kate during his last days at Mansfeld?

- Five letters are mentioned.

6. (# G) How many persons were gathered around Luther in the middle of the night on February 18, 1546?

- At least thirteen besides Luther.

7. By what process was the actual appearance of Luther's face preserved after his death?

- By the process of pressing wax on his face.

8. (# K) How many funeral services were conducted around the body of Luther?

- 3, one by Pastor Jonas, one by Pastor Coelius, and one by Pastor Bugenhagen Melanchthon gave the Latin lecture..

9. On what date and at what hour did Martin Luther die?

- On February 18, 1546, between 2:00 – 3:00 a.m.

<u>Regarding the transference of footnotes from Graebner's edition in German to the "American Edition of Luther's Works"</u>:

The listing of about 70 redirected references indicated with footnotes in the Luther biography by August Graebner is not a full listing. However, the way in which these are set up should give any reader general guidance how to proceed for for finding writings about which the original author, August L. Graebner, was providing comments or summaries.

www.ingramcontent.com/pod-product-compliance
Lightning Source LLC
Chambersburg PA
CBHW081416080526
44589CB00016B/2554